Make Your Honeymoon Last

How Your Relationship Can Remain the Perfect Love Affair

Suzie Hayman

Hodder & Stoughton
LONDON SYDNEY AUCKLAND

British Library Cataloguing in Publication Data
A record for this book is available from the British Library

ISBN 0 340 74612 2

Typeset by Avon Dataset Ltd, Bidford-on-Avon, Warks

Printed and bound in Great Britain by
The Guernsey Press Co. Ltd, Channel Isles

Hodder & Stoughton
A Division of Hodder Headline Ltd
338 Euston Road
London NW1 3BH

Thanks to Vic for being the subject of much diligent research on this matter.
Twenty-five years, still walking the talk.

Contents

Introduction

Once, you'd have walked over broken glass to see your partner and walked on air every time you did. You were Prince and Princess Charming to each other and you thought you'd live happily ever after. Now the honeymoon is over, your love life is in a rut and at times you even think the other is the pits. Don't despair, because it's possible to make your relationship one long honeymoon. However wonderful the early days of your relationship seemed, they were only that good because you were both making the effort to please each other. Make the same effort again, and the honeymoon can come back – for good. Want to know how? Read on!

We've entered the new millennium with relationships in a crisis. Marriages are falling, divorce is going up. By 2010 it is predicted that 'one marriage for life' will no longer be the pattern most people follow. Instead, living with someone, marrying or settling into what you hope will be a permanent relationship, breaking up with them and moving on to a second and even third long-term relationship or remarriage is likely to become the norm. Increasingly, we seem to want fast relationships the way we demand fast food. They have to be new, improved and 'lite'! Many of us have high, often unrealistic expectations of what to expect from a partner and what we might be required to put into a relationship. Once the honeymoon is over and the glow fades, more and more people see a solution in reaching for a new relationship rather than working at the old one.

All very depressing, most of us would agree. And what sorts of help or suggestions were we offered to deal with this situation in the last years of the old millennium? Some advisors told us the rules for how to get a date, but they didn't tell us how to keep him or her. Others told us men and women came from different planets and had different agendas. All very 90s, and not exactly the help most of us need to make lasting, real, exciting and intimate relationships. Because the truth is that, whatever century we are in, whatever our age or gender, most of us want to find and keep one special person. We long for one relationship that will last, with someone whom we can trust, rely on and love with a passion. We want a best friend who can also be a best lover. But we also want the special glow that surrounds the early days of a love affair to continue. Are length of service and passion mutually exclusive? Does excitement only go hand in hand with newness and mystery? Will it always fade as two people become used to each other?

When it comes to making and shaping relationships, playing it cool and keeping the other person guessing doesn't make you value yourself, them or the relationship. And being told you're from different species hardly helps you understand what may be going on in either of your minds. When it comes to keeping relationships going, most of us are ready and willing to hear a new message. This is that one person is better than a parade of new faces, that it is possible to find and keep them and that the key lies in understanding ourselves and our partners, and communicating with each other.

Make Your Honeymoon Last is the book for a new era. I am going to show you how to get and keep your lover, and that perfect love affair, and how to make it last. I will reveal:

- ten ways you can tell your relationship is going down the pan;
- ten ways to make your relationship bombproof;
- six things to do in bed that will transform your sex life – forever;
- five ways of saying 'I love you' without opening your mouth;
- the first three things to do when you realise you have a problem;
- the last two things to do when a row is threatening.

Other books promise the earth and rarely deliver, mainly because they make it sound so easy. Maintaining a relationship and sticking by a partner after the honeymoon is over is actually hard work. Once, marriages stayed together for life. Let's be honest, that might have had something to do with the fact that divorce was difficult to obtain so our grandparents had little choice. It was also because it was common to marry late and die early. But it may also have been because couples realised that there would be ups as well as downs, and expected to take the rough with the smooth. Now, couples do have the option of bailing out, and many do. *Make Your Honeymoon Last* will show you how to make a marriage or relationship work beyond those easy, starry-eyed first days. And *work* is the proper word, because it does take effort and time to keep a relationship going. The pay-off is how much you can benefit from long-term commitment. Readers will learn new, guaranteed and enjoyable ways to understand and make yourself understood by a partner; ways of communicating and resolving conflicts, of helping each other to make relationships and keep them. The overall aim will be to lift the lid on how successful relationships are made and kept – who we fall in love with, how and why.

Make Your Honeymoon Last is packed with inside information and striking new tactics, and is an indispensable guide to relationships in the twenty-first century. I've said boosting a relationship is hard work, but don't let that put you off – sex is hard work, too, but worth all that sweating and gasping! You can read through *Make Your Honeymoon Last* from front to back or by dipping in and out.

You can also use it as a workbook, a trigger for all sorts of discussions, games and exercises on your own or with a partner. I have tried to show how face-to-face encounters can be changed from arguments into discussions, from destructive rows into something as productive as possible. I have added strategies, tips and discussion points as well as questionnaires and quizzes to get the ball rolling. Your own active participation in this book sets the scene, because all any advisor, author or counsellor can do is help you help yourself. We can't do it for you, however much we might long to do so. Most of us have far more ability and resources than we think, and my aim is to encourage and support you in doing whatever you want and need to put your relationship on the best possible footing. It's a new century – have a renewed relationship to go with it!

1

Falling in Love

If you want a honeymoon to last, you have to go back to first principles. In other words, you need to explore what went to making that honeymoon feeling in the first place. Ask yourself, what drew you to your partner, what made you fall for them and what about them set your pulse racing? The answer will enable you to recreate, revive and prolong those feelings, for ever. Don't believe the cynics who say that if you put a mystery under the microscope you destroy it. On the contrary, knowledge is power – the power to be in control of your feelings.

Wish lists

If you could write a 'wish list' for what you wanted out of a relationship, what would it contain? We all like to think of ourselves as original and different, so some elements might be yours and yours alone. One person might deeply desire a partner who would regularly tickle their feet. Another might demand that no true love is possible unless their partner accepts their habit of midnight snacks of pickles and cheese. But most of us would come up with similar 'must-haves'. We want flirtation and romance, moonlight and roses. We want a relationship that has passion and excitement, lust and desire. We want a partner we can trust and respect, one who is honest and responsible. We want exclusivity and fidelity, to feel special and singled out. We want security and to be looked after and cosseted. We want safety and familiarity. We want to be endlessly surprised, to be thrilled and stimulated, both in and out of bed.

Don't want much, do we? But have a careful look at that list. The problem in most relationships is that there is a major contradiction in many of our needs. Most of us long for two almost mutually exclusive elements: excitement and security. Looking at the 'must-haves' you can see that they fall into two camps. We want high emotion, overwhelming desire, instant and guaranteed arousal and to be in an infatuated state of *lurve*. But we also want stability, dependability and reassurance. Mrs Patrick Campbell, a well-known wit of the 1920s, once said that 'Marriage is the result of the longing for the deep, deep peace of the double bed after the hurly-burly of the chaise longue'. It's not difficult to see that these two distinct, separate groups of emotions and behaviours – the deep, deep peace and the hurly-burly – are usually associated with two different phases of any relationship. One is the early days, the honeymoon period. When a relationship is young, that's the time when palms sweat and butterflies rocket around stomachs. That's the period in which you can virtually be guaranteed instant arousal and dynamic sex. Fear and anticipation give a boost and a spice to any emotional interaction or sexual encounter. But when the initial insanity dies down, that's the second period in which you can expect comfortable certainty and peace of mind.

However, when you listen to the love songs, watch the films or read the stories, most of them celebrate the early days. Falling in love attracts most of our attention and the rest tends to be dismissed with 'and then they lived happily ever after'. It's as if the *happily ever after* is easy and can look after itself and is less interesting and engaging than the *getting together*. This is a great pity and it is also very dangerous because it means we put less value on longevity. By not celebrating it and by not acknowledging that there are greater rewards to be found and that they do require a certain amount of effort, we leave people floundering. When the first flush of newness wears off many people feel cheated. They think 'Is this all there is to it?' They feel they have lost the only thing of value in a relationship – the feeling of excitement. Nothing much else seems forthcoming so they reach for the obvious solution which is another relationship. Start back at the beginning again with someone new and, zap, you're into fireworks and champagne time again.

So what is the best solution? To go bed-hopping, accepting that if you want a vital and sparkling relationship it has to be one that is in its infancy? Or to settle for a partnership that feels like old slippers – familiar, what you're used to, slightly shabby but comfortable? Hey, let's have some lateral thinking here. If neither option sounds just right, and it shouldn't since both are second-best, go for a third. And that's to put the magic back into a long-term relationship. To take a partnership that has gone beyond the fireworks and sparkle stage and drifted into the fireside and cocoa phase, and kick start it again. Because the fact is that you can't import all the advantages of a settled, familiar relationship into one that is just starting. If you're in the shiny-new and sweaty-palmed period, you can't expect to have total trust, deep knowledge and easy familiarity as well. But you *can* shoehorn excitement and romance back into a relationship that has a few miles on the clock.

If you want to make your honeymoon last, it doesn't come easily or without effort. It'll take commitment and resolve. The immense rewards make this worth it, though. Imagine having it all – the fizzy-tummy thrill of those first romantic and sexual encounters, but with the person you have come to trust and rely on, who knows you well enough for you not to be embarrassed or shy. So how do you go about extending those early-days' feelings for years, if not decades? The first necessity is to understand how you fall in love in the first place, with whom and why. We'll look at how we choose partners and why this may have drawn us to partners and relationships that have both the seeds of a lasting love and in-built problems.

What is this thing called love?

What exactly are love and the sensation of falling in love? Very few people go their whole lives without experiencing the turmoil of romance. Poets, songwriters, authors and artists of all types invest time and effort in trying to describe the sensations, often with little success, because although the experience is common, trying to define it is often hard. Love has been described as a chemically induced period of insanity, and one that can only last a matter of months. The phases of love, the symptoms of measles and the stages of sexual intercourse follow an identical cycle. In measles, it is infection, incubation, illness and recovery. In sexual intercourse it is arousal, plateau, orgasm and resolution. And in love it is falling in love, being in love, consummating your love and 'Ho hum, does the ceiling need painting?'

Falling in love can be like descending into a mist-filled valley where you lose your way totally. Lovers can quickly alienate their friends because no one can be more obsessive than someone in the early stages of a love affair. Your entire conversation is likely to be peppered with 'X likes that', 'X thinks this' and 'Did I tell you that X said so and so?' Falling in love can be an intensely energising and inspiring state where you rise at dawn and thrash about doing an enormous amount in a whirl of inspiration. Or it can equally trap you in a fantasy and a depression as you sit, unable to do anything but moon over the one you adore. Love can inspire you to personal achievements you never suspected you could attain or it can rob you of self-confidence and prevent you doing things you had previously taken for granted. *Falling in love* is a tremendous rush of emotions and it's not really something that is sustainable for long periods. It is usually quickly overtaken by *being in love*.

To a certain extent what you fall in love with can be a fantasy – the person that you imagine and expect and who is your dream come true. *Being in love* is a far more settled state of affairs as you get to know your partner as a genuine individual. *Being in love* may be less of an adrenalin kick but it makes up for the lack of frenetic excitement with a deeper glow. The dramatic highs may be missing but less too is the fear and insecurity of not knowing whether the person you love returns your emotion. *Being in love* is less fierce but more enduring.

Loving is the final state and it is the emotion we feel when we know a partner through and through, can see failings for what they are, and still love them.

Sexual stereotypes in our society insist that men and women see love in different ways. In fact it's been said that romance is the price men pay to get sex while sex is the price women pay to get romance. Most men would have you believe that they are interested in conquest and sex and prefer to leave the slushy stuff to the female of the species. But those who deal with men on an emotional level, such as counsellors and agony aunts, suggest that there are more similarities than differences between men and women. Women are just as interested in sex as men and men are just as helpless before the need and the tendency to fall in love. What both sexes want is intimacy and what both sexes cannot help but react to are the pangs of love.

Love at first sight

How do we fall in love? Some people say that it happened over a period of time, as a person they met or were introduced to became more than a friend or a date. But many people suggest there is such a thing as 'love at first sight'. A surprising number of people do say that there was an instant spark between them and someone with whom they subsequently have a relationship. Following on this theory, plenty of us also believe in the existence of a 'Mr/Ms Right' – that one and only person destined for each of us. The sense of 'correctness' we often feel when with the person we love seems to confirm this. The ancient Greek philosopher Plato believed that in the mists of time our ancestors were beings with four arms and four legs and two faces. Angry for some reason or other, the gods split us in half. According to Plato, the search for love was the search for your other half. Love, he felt, happened when you found and were reunited with the split section of yourself and became complete again. Belief in love at first sight and Mr/Ms Right do have some basis, and both are part of an explanation for how and why we fall in love.

Whether we realise it or not, we choose the people we fall in love with and with whom we form relationships. Falling in love, even 'love at first sight', is the result of complex decision-making rather than haphazard chance. You may think that you only have looks to go on when you catch sight of someone, or are introduced to them, and feel instantly smitten. What another person looks like is important but this doesn't mean that we fall for appearance and appearance alone. The human brain is a super-computer, able to assess and examine an amazing amount of information in less time than it takes to blink. There's a lot more to instant attraction than meets the eye. We all carry within us a blueprint of the ideal partner. When you meet or see someone, your unconscious mind spins through this checklist of desirable or essential requirements, matching up what you want and need in a partner with what you see in this person. After a certain number of ticks and crosses, you write them off or feel the glimmerings of interest. That spark can also be negative – feelings of hostility or dislike can be the start of a beautiful love affair just as much as the more obvious feelings of liking or sexual attraction. What is really interesting is that you may think only surface details can be considered this way. So you wouldn't be surprised to learn that some people have a thing about blondes with an easy smile while others go for smouldering, brooding redheads. But this blueprint can lead you to falling for less obvious characteristics, such as a tendency to cheat, a shared history of abuse or the fact that both of you lost members of your family at the same time in childhood. Such parallels in partners' backgrounds are amazingly common and frequently not realised by the couple until well into their relationship.

Mr/Ms Right

When you do meet someone who fits your blueprint there is often an intense feeling of familiarity and of their somehow fitting with you. This is where the Mr/Ms Right myth comes in. The problem with the Mr/Ms Right myth is that it encourages people to misinterpret our reactions to other people. Falling in love, establishing a relationship, marrying and having kids does not render you immune to the charms of new people. We tend to assume that if we've fallen in love, we must have found the one and only person we can pair up with. We also think that as soon as a relationship is established, it acts as a sort of vaccination against sexual or romantic attraction. You feel that no one will notice you henceforth and you certainly won't notice anyone else. This, of course, is far from the truth. When someone in a relationship finds themselves aroused by another man or woman, the myth of Mr/Ms Right leads them to believe that they got it wrong the first time. Their established partner must be Mr/Ms Wrong, the love they felt must be an illusion and they should be with the new attraction. The mistake, of course, is in thinking there will be only one person who will have this effect on you. Among all the thousands of people you will meet in a lifetime there will be a considerable number who would fit your blueprint. Just think about it – if you've a hundred points that are to be ticked or crossed, there must be many people whom you meet and know who would score in some of those categories. It's not unreasonable to expect that half a dozen people in your immediate vicinity can rack up a high enough score to hit the jackpot, even though each of them gets ticks and crosses in totally different boxes. We tend to get considerable confusion, for instance, where different people score highly in totally different if not opposed ways. For instance, one may make your pulse race but be a total user and abuser. Another produces a warm glow, because they are kindness and thoughtfulness personified. Which do you choose?

Partners and people who attract us fulfil a need, or needs, that mostly go unrecognised in our conscious minds. Often, the need is to make right something that might have gone wrong in our childhood. Events and relationships in childhood are vitally import- ant. What happens to you then is like having a script written for you, for later life. If your parents were loving and supportive, were there when you needed them but gave you plenty of encouragement to stand on your own two feet, you are likely to grow up with a script that tells you you're a worthwhile person who deserves to love and be loved. You will want to look for a partner who resembles the best in your parents. But when parents are not able to give you the care you need, and are physically or emotionally absent for all or some of your childhood, the script will be less hopeful. You'll still look for a partner who resembles a parent, but with the hope that the story will end on a happier note, with them able to love and care for you and to 'be there' for you. Sadly, you will be choosing someone like your parent in their inability to fulfil this need. And since you yourself may well have no real idea of how to satisfy the same needs in the other person, you may find yourself repeating the same mistakes your parents made with you. This is why rela- tionships, even between couples who love each other, so often break up, and why you can find other, later relationships going exactly the same way as first ones. Many of our needs remain unchanged over the years, so new partners may well resemble the old ones, both in appearances and in their characters and behaviour. They may seem different, and in some ways act differently, but unless you can come to an understanding of what you are really looking for in your partners, you may in essence go on dating, living with or even marrying the same person, and find dissatisfaction each time.

Counsellors call the way we and our partners slot together 'marital fit'. You can see it in terms of a jigsaw or the cogs of an old-fashioned clockwork watch. Your other half is the person whose pieces fit in with yours, who matches. That doesn't mean a person whose tastes are exactly the same as yours. On the contrary, it often means finding the person who fills in your gaps. Love is often more successful when you do have a lot in common, coming from similar backgrounds and therefore having similar references, but on an emotional level we often need people who match but don't accord. This is why wallflowers so often link up with party animals. One side of the partnership may have stage fright and be terrified of the thought of being the centre of attention. They fall for a partner who will do it for them – who will dance on tables, be the life and soul, for both of them. In turn, Party Animal chooses Shrinking Violet for their stability, calmness and quietness, to be the still centre of the relationship. It also explains why some men and women keep falling in love with people who use and abuse them.

The shadow of abuse

Abusive relationships are all about the need to rewrite that script. If a child grows up in a family where there is physical or emotional violence, or even where there is an apparently loving but emotionally demanding parent, it will affect how they make their own later loving relationships. Sometimes they are left with a deep sense of being unworthy. They will seek out partners who behave in much the same way as did the abusive or missing parent. They will expect nothing better from their partner because their experience has convinced them that they are worth nothing more.

Sometimes the same pattern will happen but it's because the man or woman will convince themselves that this time they can make a difference. You will find men and women who seek out unfaithful, unloving or even brutal partners or partners with addictive behaviours such as dependency on drink, drugs or gambling. Each time at the root of their love is the conviction that they can change what their partner is doing. Whether they can or not, and it's usually futile, it wouldn't make any difference because the person whose behaviour they really want to change is beyond their reach – that is, their parent. Even if they were able to make it right in the present by having their partner become as loving and caring as they want, there would still be a sense of loss. The real success, to have gone back in time and made the parent clean up their act, is impossible.

The third way that people may react in trying to rewrite their own experience of an abusive relationship in childhood is to become abusive themselves. Both men and women can visit exactly the same abuse that they suffered at the hands of their own carers upon their own partners or children. The reason for this is quite complex. You would think that if you had suffered pain and humiliation the last thing you would want to do is act that way to someone else. In fact, copying what has happened to you is a recognised coping mechanism. A child who has been hurt will feel a tremendous weight of pain, humiliation and powerlessness. The need will be to get rid of those feelings and one way of doing so is to pass them on to someone else. It's a bit like taking all your negative feelings, wrapping them in a parcel and dumping them on someone else's lap. If you can make someone else feel hurt, humiliated and powerless, you yourself can feel satisfied, strong and in control. The exact reverse, in other words, of the negative feelings you once had. This is why the abused often become abusers and why those who have been smacked and hit in childhood often become the strongest exponents of such behaviour.

The point is that children always love their parents no matter what that parent does to them – you can't help it. It's hard-wired into you and it comes with the territory. When a parent does something that makes a child feel bad two things happen. One is that the child convinces themselves that it must have happened because they did something wrong and must be at fault, which is where the conviction of unworthiness comes from. The other is that the child is driven to forgive the parent and the best forgiveness is to imitate. We defend behaviour such as smacking and do it ourselves not really because we think it's right but because we have to do so in order to forgive our parents for having done it to us. Every child wants the world to make sense and to be stable. To have to accept that our parents or carers had lost the plot and were wrong in what they did is a bit like having to accept we lived on shifting sands. It simply feels so risky we'd rather accept that it was we who were wrong and deserved what happened, however awful. People who seem unable to commit to love, or leave relationships just when the going gets good, may be reacting in another way to childhood losses. Loss is another painful experience that leaves you feeling powerless. One way of coping is to avoid being vulnerable to another person ever again, by refusing to love or by being the one who leaves first. As with abusive behaviour, the person doing it is not aware of how and why they act the way they do.

Changing the past

If the people you are likely to fall for and the way you fall in love are fixed by your childhood experiences, can you make any changes? It's usually not possible to change someone else. However hard you cry, shout or plead with another person, unless they themselves understand why they behave the way they do and want to be different, you're up against a brick wall. But anyone can change the way they feel and the way they behave. To do so, you need to understand what you do and why you do it. We are all the sum of our pasts, and all the little details of our history and our family's history go to make up the patchwork that is ourselves. Understanding these details can give you the clue to seeing where your partner fits in and why you chose each other. It can also explain the particular points of conflict you may have.

What is the point of all this dwelling on the past? Many people feel that dredging up what has happened to us, especially if it is negative or unhappy, is at best a waste of time and at worst not letting bygones be bygones. The reason it is important is that however much you might like them to do so, sleeping dogs simply won't lie. What has happened to you in your earlier life, however much you might like to ignore it, has very real effects on your present and on your future life. It won't go away just because you close your eyes. On the contrary, what it does is colour much of what you do whether you realise it or not. But the past has its strongest effect when we try and forget it because our feelings then pop up at unexpected times in unexpected ways. If you face events and your feelings about them squarely, you get them in perspective and under control.

There are several ways you can explore your own past, and that of your partner, to make sense of your relationship and any problems you might be having. One way is to construct a lifeline. Doing your own is illuminating enough. Doing one for each of you and then matching them up can be even more revealing.

Lifelines

To do a lifeline get a large sheet of paper and draw a line from left to right across the middle of it. Then mark off years from either nought to whatever age you want to go to – when you left home for instance, or from nought to your present age. On the left hand side draw a line and mark it from 0 to 10 going up from the line and from 0 to −10 going under the line. Now start your lifeline from when you were born and place yourself to begin with where you think you might have begun. For instance, if your feeling is that you were welcomed and loved and came into the world to a very positive beginning you may start your lifeline above the line at 5, 6 or wherever. If your feeling is that you came into the world to very unhappy beginnings you may want to begin below the line. If you're not sure, start on the line itself. Think of the key points and memories in your life. You might, for instance, know that at the age of 3 a grandparent you vaguely remember died and that you were confused and unhappy. You could remember that at the age of 6 you passed swimming tests at school and were overjoyed and proud. Place all the high points and low points on your chart and then join them up with your lifeline. Think over, and talk over with your partner, what the map you've produced tells you about yourself and about your attitude to your childhood.

Lisa and Barry did their lifelines together. Lisa is twenty-seven,

Lifeline Diagram

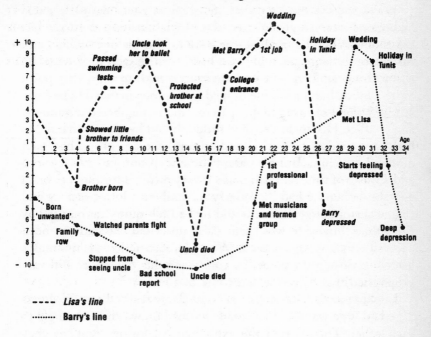

---- Lisa's line

.... Barry's line

Barry thirty-four and they have been married for five years. For the last year Barry has become increasingly depressed and their sex life has suffered as a result. Whenever Lisa tries to find out what's wrong he insists 'Nothing' and refuses to talk about it. When Lisa did her lifeline she found that most of the memories from her childhood were of events she put on the plus side of the line. She remembered being jealous and upset when her little brother was born when she was four, but that she very quickly grew fond of him and enjoyed her schooldays, particularly when she could be the big sister protecting him. The only really low point in her childhood was when, at the age of fifteen, an uncle died in a road accident. This was her mother's brother and someone she had been very fond of who used to take her out on treats and was always fun, loving and approachable. She had, in fact, gone into her profession – journalism – to follow his example.

When she showed Barry her lifeline and talked about this uncle he became increasingly agitated and eventually jumped up and left the room. When he finally came back he did his own lifeline and the reason became clear. He also had an uncle who died when he was a teenager. The difference had been that up until that point quite a lot of Barry's lifeline dipped into minus marks. He had not felt welcomed or loved by his parents and remembered arguments and conflict. His uncle also died suddenly, but by his own hand. He had been fond of this uncle and up until the age of ten had seen quite a lot of him. But his parents described him as a black sheep and a waste of time and had made it very difficult for them to be in contact. When he had died Barry remembers a lot of secrecy and shame surrounding the event and he had felt quite traumatised by the whole thing. He was particularly upset that he had not been allowed to go to the funeral. When he also followed his uncle's lead in choosing the career as a musician, his parents confidently prophesied that he too would come to a bad end.

Looking at their lifelines, Lisa and Barry realised several things together. One was the two things that had drawn them strongly to each other. They shared the experience of losing someone they loved who was an important role model at an important time in their lives. The other was the almost mirror image of their lifelines – Lisa being above the line as often as Barry was below it. In effect, they balanced each other up. The other was the fact that Barry's uncle had been twenty years older than he. In other words, he committed suicide at the age of thirty-five, the age Barry was rapidly approaching. Without realising it, Barry had become convinced that he was following his uncle's footsteps. Because he had loved and admired him he had tried to preserve his uncle's memory by becoming him. Unfortunately, that also meant he was convinced that he too was doomed to die at the same age. His parent's prophecies only added to this fear. Once Barry had understood the influence of his past upon him he could face up to his depression. Because he had missed out on properly mourning his uncle by not being allowed to go to the funeral and being forbidden to talk about him, the power of all these unspoken fears had been unbreakable. He and Lisa visited the grave and held their own wake. By talking at length about their feelings and their past Lisa and Barry found that their relationship took a dramatic turn for the better and Barry's depression faded.

Family scripts

It's important to consider the idea that much of what motivates and drives us is a script, written for us by events in our, and our family's, past. Barry was one example. Behnaz is another:

'I saw a counsellor when my second marriage was on the rocks. My husband wouldn't go so I went on my own. I found myself talking about my father a lot. I adored him, I always called him a charming rogue, which was how my mother described him. He gambled and drank and spent weeks at a time away from us, supposedly away with his job. When I was fourteen it came out that he had another woman and two more children and split his time between his families and heaven knows how many other mistresses. Well, both my husbands had been unfaithful and I was just fatalistic, thinking that that's what men did. It took counselling for me to realise that I just gravitated towards men like my father. Each time I'd hope it would be different, if I could be better or cleverer or sexier. It never was. When I looked at my relationships honestly, I could see how much each of the men I had fallen in love with over the years resembled my father. It was how they looked, or mannerisms, all sorts of things. But mostly, how they behaved. I finally realised I wasn't going to fly back in time and make it right for myself as a child so there was no point in going on saddling myself with these losers. Once I'd made that step, I fell in love again, with a man totally different to the others. We've been together fifteen years now. And, no, he hasn't been unfaithful. He's charming but not a rogue.'

Seeing the pattern set by the past as a script rather than fate or something set in stone, of course, gives you the remedy. Scripts can be rewritten. Once you know the themes that keep popping up in your life and the assumptions that are behind many of those self-fulfilling prophecies, you can change them. If you know you look for people who will let you down because you don't think you deserve better, you can work on and improve your self-esteem. If you repeatedly leave relationships just when the going gets good, you can chase down why you fear intimacy so much and do something about it.

Masks and labels

There is another part of family scripts that can become important to the way you fall in love. People within families often find themselves bearing labels that are given, or seem to be handed down, to them. These can be nicknames, descriptions or predictions. 'We call him Pigpen, he's such a messy little tyke'. Or, 'Geeta? What a joker, she's the family clown.' Or, 'Your Uncle Marty was a rebel too, and you'll end up in trouble like he did.' Sometimes the labels seem complimentary: 'She's such a good child and so helpful.' Sometimes they are more damaging: 'Your father was a no-good and you'll end up just like him.'

Imagine the roles in a family being like a set of masks for a carnival or fancy-dress costumes for a party. It's as if you have a boxful, and everybody must be dressed in one. Whether they like it or not and actually suit it or not, someone has to wear the joker, the black sheep, the clown. Once you've been handed your costume, you have to put it on and then you're stuck with it. Sometimes, you find you've had your costume chosen for you. Even if it doesn't suit you, everyone around may persist in seeing you in that light. You may end up growing to fit it because you feel you have no other choice. Sometimes you pick your own costume. You may find, even though you want to change later, nobody else can see you in any other way.

Look at these words. Can you find descriptions that fit you and your own family? Can you add any more words?

Black sheep
Little mother
Rescuer
Carer
Followers and leaders
Mother's little helper
Good child
Bad child
Rebel
Tomboy
Clown
Lazy one
Dreamer
Sulker
Little Princess
The Little Madam
Hard worker
Ne'er-do-well

Consider with your partner the roles you've assumed or been given. Do you like them? Would you like to change? How can you change? Sit down and write out a list of the beliefs you have about yourself. For every negative belief – 'I'm no good at organising', 'I'm lazy', 'I'm a useless cook' – fill in something positive – 'I'm loyal', 'I'm funny', 'I don't give up easily'. Now you have filled in your lists, think about and discuss how, when and why you got these opinions. Who told you that you were good, who told you that you were bad, and why? Were they right, and what have you done to fulfil that expectation and keep that label?

Kayleigh was always seen as the good child. She was so helpful and responsible and expected to look after her younger sister Susie, who was the naughty one. Susie was always told off for being untidy, wilful or lazy, while Kayleigh was always being praised for being obedient and hard-working. Kayleigh became a social worker, married and had two children. She spends most of her time running around after her family, who know they're not expected to lift a hand at home because good old Mum will do it all, as she always has. Susie has gone on to make a runaway success of a business that requires her to be organised, flexible and very industrious. Her family still sees her as the bad one, though. After trying to call their attention to her achievements, she's given up. Whatever she does she knows they will continue to see her as the untidy, wilful and lazy one.

Being given, and feeling you have to live up to, a 'good' label can be as destructive as being given a bad one. Either way they get you stuck in a role that you've outgrown or that stifles and undermines you. The problem with labels is twofold: they're straitjackets and they describe the wrong thing. When a person is labelled, as lazy, selfish, stupid, what is being said is that's what they are, period. They're being told they're not liked for what they are, not what they do, and thus there's no point in even trying to be different because it is them, not their behaviour, that is dislikable. When you tell yourself you are useless or incompetent or no good, you fix yourself in being like that and give yourself no hope of making any change. Why should your partner make the effort to pick up his dirty shirts, wash the pots or feed the dog? You've said that they are messy, inconsiderate and irresponsible, and cleaning up their act isn't going to change your mind about them.

The trick is to start looking at those unattractive aspects as *behaviour* rather than *person*. Not that they are *selfish* but that they are *behaving in a selfish way*. Not that they are *unhelpful*, but that they are *being unhelpful at this particular moment*. Not that they are *inconsiderate* but that *that was an inconsiderate thing to do or say*. Not that you are stupid, but that you mucked up that one time and can do better. If we stop labelling the person, we have every reason to focus on and consider changing the things that are causing problems.

Birth order

There is another aspect of family that can have dramatic effects in steering us towards one rather than another person for a relationship. Your birth order – whether you are eldest or youngest, and male or female – has a lot to do with why brothers and sisters can turn out to have such different personalities. If you're the youngest of three, you don't look at life in the same way as you would if you were an only child. If you've got two brothers, you react differently to men and women than you would if you had just one sister.

Older sisters of sisters often crave approval even though they don't mince their words and can be tactless. They may get on badly with younger or smaller women because they remind them of that pest of a sister who was always allowed to get away with everything. They may also get on badly with men who occupy the same position in the family as they did. Men with one older brother are often quarrelsome and competitive. They spent their entire childhood chasing after someone who was always one step ahead – bigger, brighter, better. They may spend their adulthood trying to catch up, while convinced they never can. So if you put an older sister of a sister with the younger brother of a brother you're bound to have a quarrelsome relationship.

Women with older brothers may also spend their lives trying to catch up, because they've grown up in the shadow of someone bigger and stronger. They can react badly to criticism and instead of listening and trying to do better they may argue and defend themselves. They can be 'economical with the actualitie', lying about being given praise or a promotion at work. They tend to want a contradiction – an assertive husband who will do what he is told. A man who has older brothers or/and sisters would have a successful relationship with a woman with older brothers, as neither would remind the other of the overbearing behaviour of their siblings.

Men with sisters get on best with women, especially with those who've had older sisters. Younger sisters often feel the elder had a better deal of it and are still jealous of her and by extension, any older woman. They may get on best with a man who's had sisters of his own. Only children of either sex are leaders, make good friends but don't forgive disloyalty easily and can be very ambitious. Since they've never had to compete for attention they tend to grow up to be more generous and less demanding and selfish than those who have brothers and sisters. When it comes to partners, they get on best with another only child and women may also prefer their partners to be quite a bit older than them.

Middle children tend to get forgotten. The oldest has special duties and the youngest is fussed over while they beaver away in silence. They keep quiet if people hurt them. They keep quiet if people please them. Then, occasionally, they can drop a bombshell by announcing what's been on their mind for months or years. They stick by those who have earned their friendship and they hate favouritism, probably because they've watched it go on in their family too often. They also stick to the rules, whether it's a game or real life. They won't be unfaithful and expect the same from their partner in return, which is why they may find it very hard to forgive infidelity. They're one of the few people who can get on with a partner from any position in a family – because they are prepared to change to fit in with anyone.

Older sisters of brothers are likely to be organisers and a peace-makers. Hardly surprising, they've had plenty of practice! Because of the fuss that's so often made over boys they probably had to take a back seat when a brother came along and they made up for it by looking after him – and pushing him around. They're happiest in male company, although may have a few close girlfriends. Since they can look after themselves, they hate men who fuss over them, and probably choose a partner who respects them and gives them their head. Younger brothers or only children suit them well.

The more brothers and sisters you have, the more difficult it is to work out your birth order and what this means. A boy with an elder sister is likely to grow up selfish and carefree, able to wrap girls round his little finger and take great pride in it. The more older sisters he has, the worse the condition can get. The oldest in such a family will always be the steady one: the larger the family the more used he or she will be to taking responsibility. Youngest children, on the other hand, get used to being looked after by everyone else and can be spoilt and irresponsible. But in some cases, large families 'split up'. If you have two older brothers and a younger sister, and the boys are much older than you, you may think and act as if you only had a sister, while they grow up as if each only had a brother. Or you and one of the boys may act as brother and younger sister − leaving the other boy to act as a middle child and your sister as an only child.

One way of tracing and understanding the influences your family and childhood had and still have on your relationship, is to construct a genogram of your partnership. A genogram is a dynamic family tree. Just as in an ordinary family tree, you chart each member of the family but with the addition of noting something significant about them.

Family trees

Family trees are usually ways of showing who is related to whom. When you use them to explore your background, they can give you a surprisingly clear picture of how you feel about yourself and your own place in a family, and how you feel about other people, too. To do this, you draw a diagram of your family, but as well as names, ages and where everyone fits in the family, you add little 'word sketches' of everybody. As well as showing that you have an aunt called Shirley who was your mother's eldest sister, you can note that she was a cold and controlling person who always put her younger sister down; or that she was a warm, loving person you remember took you to pantomimes at Christmas. Family history, and family secrets, can emerge and these begin to show you the patterns that form your family script. You often find that 'themes' crop up which can give you clues to how and why your relationship flourishes or flounders.

One warning about doing a genogram. This exercise can be startlingly powerful. However well you think you know your family, you are almost certain to make discoveries. Not just about what

Doing a genogram

Get a large sheet of paper. Use these symbols to draw up your chart:

Woman

Man

Married couple

Unmarried couple

Separated couple

Divorced couple

Children of couple

[A]   (F)

Adopted; fostered children

Person who has died

m. 10·3·87
Date of marriage

d. 11·6·93
Date of divorce

55
Age at present

Age at death

happened, but about significance and patterns. Some of these may be surprising, many of them could be eye-opening, but a few could be painful. By putting it all down on paper and thinking about your background, you're going to make connections and make some sense about matters that might have simmered under the surface for years. Make sure you do this exercise with some back-up, preferably with someone you trust, when you are feeling safe and supported.

Put yourself and your current partner at the centre of the page, and then draw in your own parents, your brothers and sisters (if any). While you are filling in all the facts, add impressions and what comes to mind about all these people and about yourself. Put down what pops into your mind while you are doing this, without stopping to think whether it is relevant or not, because the things your memory allows to rise to the surface often have the most importance.

If you find yourself stuck and need some prompts, look at this list and make a note of which words strike a chord. Are there any that you feel could be applied to you or anyone in your family? Are there any that make you feel anxious, angry or intrigued?

abuse
adoption/fostering
anger
behaviour
birth order (oldest, middle, youngest etc.)
carers and rescuers
closeness/distance (physical and emotional)
deaths and losses
drink
drugs/pills
eating problems
family stories

fears
friction and conflict
illness
infidelity
jealousy
job/career
martyrs
medical history
money
moods and depression
myths and mysteries
nicknames
optimists and pessimists
perfectionists and 'slap-happys'
roles – black sheep, little mother, clown
secrets
separation/divorce
stresses and pressure
teasing
temperament
traditions
trust
violence, in and outside the family
wallflowers and party animals

You could also chart the strength of feeling between certain people – who's close, who's distant, who has a stormy relationship. Use these lines to show:

| Closeness | ===== | These two people love each other and are caring and supportive. |
| Conflict | ∿∿∿ | These two people do not get on well together. |

Smothering	≡≡≡	These people have a relationship that could be described as close and special, but it's too close. They smother each other, or one smothers the other, and are unable to distance themselves.
Distance	• • •	These two people go out of their way to avoid each other and are indifferent to each other.
Estranged	–//–	These two people may appear to be distanced but in fact the very strength of their antagonism suggests there is still a strong link between them. They deny this by running away from each other, and refusing to examine what caused the break up.

Now look at what you have drawn and written into your own genogram. Can you see any patterns or themes that repeat and might have a message for you now?

For instance, when Tim and Clare did their genogram, they found some startling parallels in their backgrounds. These went a long way to explaining problems they had been having.

Tim and Clare had a new baby. Clare went back to the home she had shared with Tim immediately after the birth, but soon after moved back to her mother's home and stayed. She found it difficult to explain why but said she found it hard to rely on Tim, although she couldn't come up with any concrete reasons for any lack of trust in him. For his part, Tim was desperate to keep Clare and their baby and was in despair at their leaving. He felt Clare's mother was making it very hard for him to see them or to prove his commitment to them. He made frequent visits which ended in

Tim and Clare's genogram

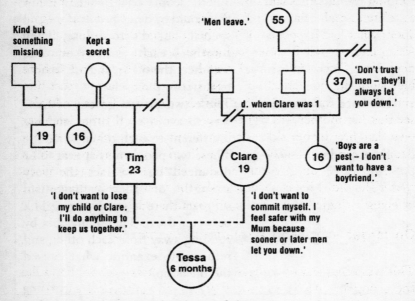

Kind but something missing

Kept a secret

'Men leave.' 55

'Don't trust men – they'll always let you down.' 37

d. when Clare was 1

19 16

Tim 23

Clare 19

16 'Boys are a pest – I don't want to have a boyfriend.'

'I don't want to lose my child or Clare. I'll do anything to keep us together.'

'I don't want to commit myself. I feel safer with my Mum because sooner or later men let you down.'

Tessa 6 months

stand-up rows between the three of them.

The genogram threw up several interesting items. Clare's father had left soon after she was born, and her grandfather had done the same soon after Clare's mother was born. Tim's mother had recently admitted the man he thought was his father was actually a step-father. Tim's birth father had deserted both of them a matter of weeks after he had been born. His mother was married a year later to the man he had been brought up to consider his father, but had always known there was a secret that nobody wanted to discuss. Both Tim and Clare had, in effect, been brought up with this shared message, that men don't stay when a new baby comes along. Clare had 'gone home to mother', and mother had kept her there, because both were convinced that men couldn't be trusted; better to leave them and manage on your own than to give them the chance to let you down. Tim in his turn was desperate to keep his baby in an effort to rewrite his own story. He felt that, somehow, if he stayed loyal and by the side of his own son, it would be as if his real father had stayed true to him. Once both of them realised they were running on tramlines laid down by the past, rather than being able to relate to each other as individuals, they were able to think again about what had happened. When he accepted that nothing he did was going to alter his own sadness at his past, Tim became less desperate. Once she realised that her grandfather's and father's behaviour did not reflect on Tim's, Clare could learn to trust him and not to be influenced by her mother's cynicism. Clare could also see that her mother was trying to come between them to keep her own daughter by her side as a consolation – men may leave but a daughter can be persuaded to stay. Clare's grandmother was still a powerful force and presence in her mother's life. Clare realised that if she didn't break the circle, she too would follow the pattern of being a single parent with no long-term relationships.

On target – drawing a relationship map

This is another way of understanding the patterns in your life. Like the genogram, it's an exercise that can give you some surprising insights; it can be exciting but it can also be powerful and thus upsetting. So take care and try to do this exercise in a supportive situation with the opportunity to talk it over afterwards with family or friends. You can do it with your partner, agreeing to take turns (spin a coin for who goes first), to listen and be sympathetic, or you can do it on your own.

Drawing the circle
Get a large sheet of paper and some pens and draw a series of circles, one inside the other – like a target or bull's-eye. Cast your mind back to your childhood and pick an age – 10, 13, 8, whatever. The age that pops into your mind is likely to be the one you will learn something from recalling.

Remember yourself at that age and put yourself, at that age, in the centre of your circles. You can put a dot labelled

---

with your name or draw a little picture or stick diagram to show yourself. Then, think of all the people you had a relationship with at that time – your parents, brothers and sisters, grandparents, aunts and uncles, friends and anyone connected with you in some way. You can include 'missing' people such as parents who live apart, too. Put all of them on your map, with the ones to whom you felt closest emotionally, nearest to you. For instance, if you got on with your Mum, you might put her in the centre with you or in the next circle. If you had a distant relationship, you'd put her way out on the edge. Resist putting people where you think they should have been or would like them to have been. The point is to show yourself the picture as it really felt. Relationship maps show emotional closeness, not physical closeness. You may, therefore, find yourself putting someone you only saw once a week or far less right next to you on the map while someone you saw every day goes out on the edge.

When you have placed all your family, look at how you have arranged them. The way you have laid them out says a lot about how you feel. Did you find it hard to place some people? Who was close to you? Who did you see as closer or farther away than you expected? Who was closer or farther away than you might have liked? Was there anyone there you didn't want at all, or is there anyone not on the map you might have liked to be there? Are you surprised at where you have put some of your contacts?

If you had the power to make one change in this pattern, what would it have been? Why? Finally, think about what you might learn from the pattern you made. Is there any likeness to the pattern you see in your childhood and what is going on now?

Liam and Siobham saw a counsellor for help because their relationship seemed to be going through a rough patch. They had been together for five years and Siobham wanted them to get married.

Siobham's relationship map

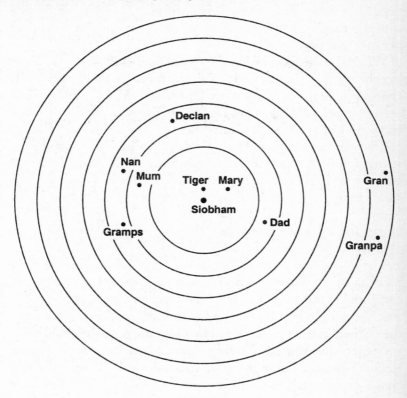

Liam was less keen, saying that the relationship worked fine as it was. What was the point of marriage, he said, since they didn't plan to have children for the moment and there was plenty of time to think of a wedding if and when they did. Siobham felt Liam had withdrawn from her and become less affectionate since the subject had come up. Liam felt Siobham had become demanding and complaining. They did a relationship map with their counsellor to look at their family backgrounds.

When Siobham did her map, she chose to do it for her family when she had been nine years old. She put both her parents one circle away from herself, but on opposite sides. She put her sister next to her and her brother two circles away, nearer their mother than their father. She put her maternal grandparents side by side with her mother, her father's parents on the very outer rim – and her cat right next to her.

When she was asked what she would do if she could have made any change, Siobham looked at the map for some time before sadly saying, 'Leave it as it is – or move Dad next to Mum.' Siobham had been nine years old when her Dad left to live with another woman, and soon lost touch with his first family. When she looked at the pattern she had made, Siobham suddenly realised that how she felt at that moment about her relationship with Liam was exactly the way she had felt as a nine-year-old. Siobham had realised long before then that her parents' marriage was in trouble, but she hadn't been able to admit it to herself or talk about it openly. What she longed for, every day, was to hear them say they had worked it out.

Once he was gone, she waited for him to get back in contact and to say he was sorry and loved them best of all. And here she was again, waiting for a declaration of love and commitment, convinced that if he didn't say he loved her and prove he wanted to stay, the man in her life was bound to leave sooner or later. Once she realised that, she understood that in some ways she could never get what she wanted. Forcing Liam to make a commitment wouldn't work, because it wasn't Liam she wanted to make that choice but her father, and the time for that was long past. But because she now saw that much of her unhappiness was from leftover feelings from the past, Siobham was able to separate those from her anxieties about the present. She was able to value herself more and see that Liam loved and wanted her and could and would stay with her, even without the public declaration of marriage.

Liam was then able to talk to her about his own family. His parents had recently celebrated their thirtieth wedding anniversary. He loved them, but his main feeling about his own childhood had been that he and his sister stood between their parents, holding them together. His parents were seen by all their, and his, friends as the perfect couple, but to Liam there was precious little love or affection at the heart of the relationship. Marriage, to Liam, was all about appearances. What made him avoid marriage to Siobham was the fear that once wed, their partnership would also dwindle into habit and neglect.

Getting control

If you think of falling in love as just 'something that happens', out of the blue, you can be forgiven for feeling that it's a situation out of your control. You'd then also feel that once love changes and appears to die, that too would be something about which you were powerless. Perhaps now you can see that love isn't random, which also means that with a bit of understanding, you can be in the driving seat. Once you can grasp the foundations of your own relationship, you can shore them up if they've got a bit shaky. If you want to keep your relationship alive, you can also use your knowledge to return to those first principles whenever you choose.

There is another reason for going back to remembering what it was that attracted you to your partner. Analysing is important, because it allows us to be in charge of our feelings and what we do about them. But sometimes it's also just important to *feel*.

Recalling the past

If you and your partner have lost the plot and your relationship has become flat and stale, try this. Get back in touch by taking the time to recall the emotions you had for them in the early days.

Sit down with your partner and tell him or her:

- what you first noticed about them;
- what attracted you first to them;
- what you liked doing with them when you first knew each other;
- what you miss doing and would like to do again;
- what you like doing now;

> • what new thing you'd like to do with them.
>
> Make a date, this weekend or one evening this week, to do one of the things you miss doing from the past, like doing now or would like to try. Agree to do this exercise once a week in future. Take it in turns to choose something old or new to keep your relationship alive.

You may feel those emotions are long gone and that such an exercise would be just going through the motions. Well, here's the carrot: you'd be surprised how feigning an emotion swiftly becomes feeling that emotion. This is one of the reasons I'm always so strongly against people 'playing it cool' and not being up-front and honest about how they feel for someone. Playing cool is playing with fire, of course, because of the dangers of simple misunderstanding. Some people may be fired up to pursue when they think you're unobtainable, but just as many would take the hint, think you're not interested and withdraw. Your disdain can spark off similar feelings in them. But perhaps the most important reason against playing it cool is that when you play cool, you often go cool. Conversely, when you play hot, especially when it's to call to mind very real feelings you once had, you soon find they're there for real again. Once the early, sparkly days are over, the problem is that both of you may be driving each other down a spiral of indifference. You're not interested, so neither is your partner, which in turn hardly inspires you. So summon up that past enthusiasm, talk about it, describe it, wallow in it. You may find it soon takes over and runs away with you.

Part of the problem of losing the honeymoon feeling may be to do with losing touch with our original emotions. Getting them back is possible by exploring and understanding how and why we fell in love. But many of the problems in relationships come about because we have highly unrealistic expectations of love and partnership. There are a host of harmful myths that affect the way we maintain our relationships. In the next chapter we'll look at all the myths and fantasies we might have about relationships, and how we can overcome them.

2

Expectations

It's very easy to drift into a long-term and loving relationship with the impression that 'It just happens'. We think just getting married or settling into a long-term relationship will give us all the know-how and skills to be the perfect couple. The reason for this impression is pretty obvious. Look around you, and the message seems to be that making relationships is an art you're born with, not a skill you learn. Nobody seems to be saying 'This isn't an easy job, there are things you need to know and we're going to tell you how.' Where, after all, do we learn about making relationships? We certainly don't do so in schools. Up to now most personal or sexual education has tended to concentrate on reproduction. Guidelines for schools emphasise the importance of marriage and family life. What schools are not required to do is tell you exactly how to go about the nuts and bolts of establishing and developing relationships. We tend to learn how to be in a relationship by watching it at first hand, from our own families. Experiential learning in this case may not be much help.

If your parents' relationship is not a good one, what you may learn from them is that couples argue and bring each other down. If theirs is a relationship without closeness you will learn that intimacy is frightening and dangerous. If theirs is a relationship in which communication is poor, you learn that partners keep their worries, fears and feelings to themselves and then complain because their partner doesn't understand them. But even if you are lucky enough to have parents who have a loving and strong relationship, their example may not give you enough clues as to how to achieve that yourself. Their behaviour will show you the fruits of their labours, but by the time you are old enough to learn from them they'll already have passed through much of the groundwork. You may get the impression that the sort of closeness they enjoy is a god-given right or something that just comes naturally. You won't realise how much effort you have to put into it. The problem with picking up information and impressions without actually discussing it or putting it to the test is that this can set up very unrealistic expectations.

The myth of true love

What unrealistic expectations do many of us have when we think about loving relationships? One expectation which can be less than helpful is that of 'true love'. We promote the myth that for a relationship to be real, lasting and genuine it must be the only one. Gone perhaps are the days when we expected our partners to be virgins and not to have had any sexual experience with other people, but we still tend to insist that they shouldn't have been in love before us. The fear is that you can only fall in love, truly, once. This means that we feel the need to run down previous lovers and demand from our partners that they do the same. It's hardly helpful to start a new relationship on what may often be a lie because it makes us feel guilty. It can also make us doubt the validity of what we have.

Don't forget that the passions of your teenage years, especially the first time you fell in love, have a particular intensity purely because it was a new experience. Adult amours may never quite come up to the violence of those earlier emotions. Later loves have far more depth, but if you are going to be judging this all on the basis of a belief that 'true love' only strikes once, you may find yourself deciding that the heights are all behind you. As an agony aunt I get many letters from people who say they think they made a mistake in marrying someone because now all they can think about is their first love. What has often happened is that the initial flush of love has faded with a new partner and the contrast of what they are feeling now with what they felt then leads them to believe they have made a mistake. They think that if they go back to the first person it will all be moonlight and roses again. Belief in 'true love' can also trip you up even when your relationship is a happy one. It can come as some surprise to find yourself still attracted to other people. Many affairs start simply because one member of a couple fell for someone else and thought it meant they had fallen out of love with their partner and in love with someone new, and had to follow through on it.

The fact is that however passionately you are in love with your partner you are still going to notice and be attracted to other people, as they are to you. That wedding ring or that declaration of a partnership does not cast an invisible protective shield around you, protecting you from the outside world and the outside world from you. And nor should it, because relationships are not about being the only two people left in the world. After all, what value is love if it's not a choice? Having been in love before and having the capacity to be attracted by and to other people does not invalidate the strength or reality of being in love now. On the contrary, it means two things. One is that you are offering to your partner the statement that you are with them by choice and decision, not because there is nowhere else to go or that you don't have the experience to make a different judgment. The other is that you are bringing to your relationship the ability to love. What, after all, are you saying if you expect a partner in their mid-twenties to have never been in love before? You would be requiring them to be a pretty stunted human being.

Steady state theory

Perhaps the most damaging expectation in a new relationship is what I'll call 'Steady state theory'. Most of us spend a lot of our childhood and much of our teenage years looking forward to being an adult. We are constantly informed that we inhabit a sort of anteroom – a waiting phase that leads up to the real thing. We are always being told we can't do certain things until we are older or that we must do certain things in order to prepare for when we are older. The endless refrain seems to be 'You'll understand when you are older and you'll thank me when you are older. Just wait until you are older.' Very few young people are encouraged, or have the opportunity, simply to enjoy their childhood and adolescence. It's seen as a passing experience with the goal of adulthood. This means it's hardly surprising we come to think of adulthood as being a destination – a place, a steady state. Once you are grown up you think you'll know things, be able to go places, be able to choose what to do. You will have reached 'There'.

All of this sets you up to believe once you've fallen in love and made a relationship with someone, that's it. Everything thereafter is set in stone. You don't expect yourself to change, your partner to change or your relationship to change. Which means you don't prepare for any differences to come along and can become highly confused when they do. If you thought about it logically, you'd realise the flaw in this belief. Childhood and adolescence lasts less than twenty years. Adulthood, if we're going by the biblical, 'three score years and ten', lasts another 50 years – and possibly 80 years in the future. Just because what appears to be the most obvious physical alterations seem to occur during our first twenty years, as we grow from a single cell to a foetus to a baby, a child and a teenager, that hardly means our bodies don't change over the subsequent years. We may not grow taller, but we can certainly grow fatter, skinnier or shrink as old age advances. Our appearance, in fact, alters dramatically. But by the same token, our inward self can become very different over the years. And this means our relationships can alter too. Recognising, celebrating and being prepared for change is what adulthood is all about. This is also what good relationships are really about.

A common mistake that can lead to tremendous strains and difficulties in a modern, westernised relationship is the view that each member of a couple should be all things to their partners. It's probably an understandable contrast to the old days of what were virtually arranged marriages. In the past the main function of a marriage was for families to come together and support each other. Passionate love was often not on the agenda, but alliances were. A couple were primarily expected to give to each other comfort and aid. Instead of being a romantic one-to-one it was seen as being a group thing. You came together, with several generations, to have plenty of children and you expected to get companionship from all members of the family, not just from your partner. Today in western culture, we see our romantic relationships as being most of all about love and sex. More than that, we also see them as being our main source of friendship, entertainment, stimulation and much else. We may have firm friendships during our teenage years and in our early twenties, but many people assume that as soon as love walks in the door the need for anyone else walks out. This means we load an awful lot onto our lovers. Not only must they satisfy us sexually and romantically, they must also keep us entertained, informed, comforted, supported and amused. And if we do show a hankering for a night out with the girls or the boys, or to see old friends again, the fear often is that one partner is somehow failing in not being able to keep the other interested.

Sexual expectations

Our sexual lives probably suffer more than any other aspect of relationships from unrealistic expectations. There are a host of myths that really hamper good communication here. One is that you are born knowing how to do it and you don't have to learn. In fact sex (whether we are talking about understanding your sexual feelings, giving yourself sexual pleasure or giving someone else sexual pleasure) is just like any other skill or behaviour in life. That is, it's something you have to learn and to practise. The problem with sexual skills is that, unlike walking, talking or riding a bicycle, these are not skills that your parents or teachers seem particularly keen to pass on or encourage you to acquire. When we are very young we set about learning skills with a will. Small babies and children explore their own bodies and find out pretty quickly that if you touch that, stroke this and twiddle with several other bits you get a rather pleasurable result. While the adults around will enthusiastically support your attempts at learning to walk or talk, this struggle will attract a slap, a 'tsk, tsk' or a hurried distraction. Pretty quickly you will get the impression that touching yourself is both embarrassing and wrong and that your body and sexual pleasure is rather dirty and unpleasant. Once you start asking questions you may find that the subject is changed or that you get told off when you venture into this area. You soon get the message that sex is not something to be talked about openly. So it's altogether hardly surprising that when we settle down with a sexual partner we feel shy, tongue-tied and awkward. We can't talk about what we are doing or how we are feeling because we know it's all rather sordid and unsavoury. We feel we have to get it right or be shown up as an idiot; we can't ask how we are doing in case, yet again, we get told off as we were when we were young. Above all, the general silence persuades us that since nobody else is asking questions they must know what they are doing.

Mind-reading

Couples often think they should be mind-readers, able to know how their partners feel and what they want or need. Part of the getting-to-know-you process is learning your partner's tastes and foibles. In a sense the whole point of a relationship is that you are familiar with and indeed have intimate knowledge of the other person. One of the joys of a good partnership is that you do know a lot about the person you live with – the food they like, the clothes they prefer and the sorts of things they enjoy doing. The mistake we often make is to go that one extra mile and assume that because we know much about them, we have total and absolute knowledge. Particularly, the problem is that such assumptions don't allow for the fact that we all grow and change. If you haven't realised that you need to keep talking and to keep checking you are stuck only with the information you learnt about your partner when you first got together. You are also stuck when it comes to areas which you haven't fully discussed. The most glaringly obvious of these may be your sex lives.

Men and women often feel too shy to talk explicitly about what turns them on and turns them off. They'll look for clues in the way their partner seems to behave or, most frequently and misguidedly, they will listen to the myths and stereotypes of male and female sexuality. I get a lot of letters to my agony page that contain the same theme. They complain that their sex lives are far from satisfactory and that their partners feel inadequate for not being able to 'give them' an orgasm. They frequently have a pretty good idea of what would do the trick but feel utterly unable to tell their partners what to do. Their belief is that their partner should know. The reality is that even a sexually experienced man or woman may not have the foggiest idea what a particular partner may find arousing. We are all individuals, not just out of bed but in it too. A previous partner may have adored murder mysteries, chocolate mousse and having their nipples tweaked – that doesn't mean to say the present one has the same tastes. Because we all like different things, we all respond to different things and we can't read our partner's mind. The importance of sharing and discussing cannot be over-estimated.

Beginner's mind

Do I know you? Of course, you're the guy who hates being interrupted when he's watching the news, who has to have roast potatoes, not mashed or boiled, with his chicken and who wouldn't come to the salsa class with me in a month of Sundays. And you know me. I'm the one who hates exercise, would never wear dangling earrings and who loathes getting wet in the rain.

We all tend to build up a picture of our partners over the months and years we've been with them. The problem is that those assumptions often stop us from seeing what is really going on or trying anything new.

Sandy and his partner Geoff, for instance, felt they knew each other very well. Sandy knew there was no point in trying to get Geoff out of a bad mood after they'd had a row because Geoff always retreated behind a newspaper and wouldn't talk. It wasn't until a friend asked Sandy how he 'knew' that there was no point in persisting that he approached the situation in a new light. Looking at their relationship with what is called the 'beginner's mind' he questioned what was going on.

Beginner's mind is a Zen phrase for seeing everything with fresh eyes instead of in the way you've grown to look at it. It means, in effect, being like a two-year-old and taking nothing for granted and asking 'Why?' to every single response.

When Sandy looked at the situation with beginner's mind he realised that he was operating on assumptions formed in the first year of their living together. Because Geoff rebuffed his first advances the first time they had a row, he'd always assumed there was no point in going any further. When he looked carefully, with better knowledge of his partner, he realised what Geoff wanted more than anything else was to be coaxed out from behind his newspaper. When Sandy, instead of leaving him there, challenged him and insisted on talking, Geoff eventually came out and was able to talk things over and put the row to rest.

If you 'know' how your partner will react, and your partner 'knows' how you will, there's no point in talking. Just because we've done it one way once doesn't mean we wouldn't want to be different next time. Geoff was sulking because he felt unloved and unlistened to. He wanted – indeed, needed – to have Sandy make an effort. Both were actually longing to make up and talk, and each assumed the other didn't care.

Next time you find yourself doing, or not doing, something because you *know* how your partner will act, try 'beginner's mind'; look at it with fresh eyes, ask yourself how you can be sure of what you think you know, and *ask*. It may mean you end up serving rice, changing your hair style or learning how to cycle in the rain. Who cares – it may mean you end up talking.

Introductions

Now that you've assumed a beginner's mind, it's time to get to know each other. Think about it – haven't your feelings changed about a lot of things since you first got together? Odds are you don't wear the same clothes or have the same hair style. And it's likely that you think differently about many issues, because your relationship has changed and you've changed with it. But your partner may be working on the assumption that you still want the things you said you did when you first met. Why not take the time to reintroduce yourselves to each other? Talk about what's important to you now, what you want to do, where you want to go, what would make your life satisfying. Listen to your partner tell you about how s/he feels about these things. Find out how your partner views him/herself now, what matters most, what s/he really wants out of the years to come. Listen without criticising or judging, and even if you hear things that scare the pants off you, accept what your partner is saying as being true for them. You don't have to like everything you hear; you just have to be willing to see things as they are at this moment. Remember, this is not a negotiation session. It's a 'getting-to-know-you' conversation. Let yourself be curious and surprised.

Introduce yourself

A good way of starting Introductions is to think about and tell each other some favourite things. Sit down with a pad and pencil. Separately, write down your favourite:

colour
film
music
TV programme
clothing
possession
book
sport (to watch and/or to do)
pet
season/time of year
time of day
food
drink
best holiday
worst holiday
way to spend a Sunday afternoon

Share these with your partner and see if there are any surprises.

If you and your partner are to have a happy and positive life together, you need to understand what you expect from your relationship, yourselves and each other. If you're not getting or giving what you expect, you might be feeling let down, cheated or inadequate. Such destructive emotions are often at the bottom of arguments between couples. But there's no point in trying to change yourselves or your partner if what may be at fault is your expectation.

Expectations

Sit down with your partner with a pad of paper and a pen/pencil. Ask yourselves these three questions:

What do I expect from a partner?
What do I expect from myself?
What do I expect from a relationship?

The sorts of ideas you might find yourself putting down could be:

What do I expect from a partner?
They'd love me, no matter what.
I'd be the first person they ever loved.
I wouldn't have to tell them I was feeling sad, happy, sexy – they'd just know.
My partner would always put me first.
They'd be faithful to me.
They'd look after me.
I could rely on them.
They'd be expert in bed.
They'll always be interesting.
They'll have no secrets from me.

What do I expect from myself?
I'd be in charge.
I'd always be attracted to my partner.
I'd always want sex with my partner.
I'll know how to make love.
I'd know how to communicate with my partner.
I'll know how to be a good partner.

What do I expect from a relationship?
We'll be a couple.
I'd be safe and loved.

I'd always have someone to care for me.
I wouldn't need any other people.
It will last for ever.
It will never change.
We'll have children.

When you've added your own ideas, talk them over with your partner. Are your expectations realistic? Where did you learn to expect these things? Are they helping or hindering you and your partner in making a happy relationship?

When Jan and Rich did their list of expectations, Jan says:

'I put down that I expected that I could rely on my partner. When we talked it over I realised this was all about my Dad. He left when I was nine and used to see me and my brother but he was so cavalier about arrangements and you could never, ever depend on him. When I looked at it, I realised I expected exactly the opposite, that you couldn't rely on other people. And in fact, I'd become someone who took charge and made sure arrangements were kept. Rich is a lovely guy but he's a bit slapdash and "Oh, I'll do that tomorrow". We used to have dreadful rows with me complaining that he never did things. When I looked at what I said I expected and what I really expected, I could see that I was saying one thing because that's the way it's supposed to be, i.e. men taking charge. But what I really wanted was for me to do it so I'd know it gets done. Now I've thrown this "men have to be the ones who do it all" stuff overboard, we get along much better.'

Talking

Once we've unpicked what we expect from our relationships, the next stage is to talk about it to our partners. But this is easier said than done. We learn how to talk as children. We string words together and gradually improve our ability to make ourselves understood. It's easy to feel therefore that communication is just something you get on with and know how to do. While most of us can talk, surprisingly few of us have had the opportunity to learn how to communicate confidently, expertly or easily. Communication skills are not something we learn from school and often it's not something that our own parents have passed on to us. The difference between talking and communicating is that communicating is two-way. It's not just a question of getting someone to listen to you, you also have to know how to listen to them, and listening is a lot more than just shutting your mouth and opening your ears.

We tend to see the main goal of a conversation as getting ourselves understood, and we see that as being the same as getting our own way. We often don't want to hear the other person's point of view in case we are swayed by their viewpoint and they win. But communication isn't about persuasion, it's about agreement. It's not about one person's idea overriding the other's – about one person winning and the other person losing. True communication should lead to what Americans call a 'win–win scenario' and what financiers call a 'non-zero-sum game'. If you listen and the other person listens, if you talk and the other person talks, both of you are likely to end up feeling that you've been heard and have heard the other point of view. You will then find there will be a degree of understanding and satisfaction before you even move into talking about results. If you are making decisions on the basis of all this talk, the chances are that neither of you is going to get exactly what you wanted, but neither of you is going to get none of what you wanted. You will get a negotiated compromise with a bit of both, and the chances are you may not even be able to remember which was yours and which was theirs.

> Love is always having to say sorry, please and thank you.

Love, far from being 'never having to say you're sorry' (perhaps the most stupid, destructive and pernicious notion ever to be promulgated by Hollywood!), is always having to say everything. It doesn't matter how much you love each other or how much you'd like to get along together; if you don't communicate clearly, misunderstandings and difficulties are bound to affect your relationship, for the worse. Our behaviour frequently passes messages that may be at odds with what we would really like to say. More importantly, our own beliefs about what is going on may prevent us understanding the other person's point of view. Look at this dialogue between Leona and Wayne. Is this a situation you can recognise?

	What s/he said	How it came over	What s/he was thinking	What s/he really felt
Leona	Let's go out tonight, Wayne.	No time to sit around, let's go, let's go!	I've had a hard week and I really could do with a treat.	Tired, fed up.
Wayne	Ah, do we have to?	Yo, man, all I want to do is veg out.	Here she goes again! She just wants to see her friends, she doesn't want to spend any time with me.	Passed over.
Leona	Oh, come on, you never want to do anything!	Snappy, critical.	If he had his way we'd stay in all the time. What's up, he ashamed to be seen with me?	Cheated and rejected.
Wayne	That's not true, I took you out last Sunday.	Last of the big spenders.	She makes me feel two inches tall when she gets at me like this.	Got at.
Leona	Oh, yeah, to the pub to see your mates and watch you play pool.	As if I'd enjoy a night out with you and your friends.	He spent most of the night with his mates at the bar, ignoring me.	Spurned and worthless.

	What s/he said	How it came over	What s/he was thinking	What s/he really felt
Wayne	I thought you liked them, they're our friends, not just mine, aren't they?	Petulant	I thought she was having a good time talking to her friends. If she didn't like it, why didn't she say?	Miserable.
Leona	That's just not my idea of a night out.	Spoiling for a fight.	I just want to spend some special time, alone, with you.	Frustrated.
Wayne	Fine, you go and do whatever you think is fun and I'll stay here.	Doesn't want to know.	It always ends in a row when I don't do what she wants.	Miserable.
Leona	Oh, come on Wayne, don't be such a wet blanket. What's the matter?	Let down your guard and I'll use it against you.	What did I do wrong this time?	Panic.
Wayne	Nothing's the matter. I'm fine.	Who needs you?	I feel miserable, isn't it obvious? She shouldn't have to ask, she should know.	Even more miserable.
Leona	Well, excuse me for asking!	Furious – don't expect to get back in my good books for ages.	I tried my best and this is what I get.	Hurt.

	What s/he said	How it came over	What s/he was thinking	What s/he really felt
Wayne	Don't bother.	So who gives a damn.	All I wanted was to start the weekend on the sofa, alone together. She's gone off me.	Unmanned, unwanted.

Leona and Wayne could have ended their conversation on a very different note, if one or both of them had used communication skills to convey and understand the hidden dialogue going on behind their words. To communicate truly with someone else, you have to be prepared, willing and able to do several things. First, you may need to understand what is stopping you from understanding each other. Before you can make changes so you can talk more easily, it helps to understand what may be holding you back.

> Perhaps the most important barrier to communication is simply the fact that we may not have learned how. Knowing how to communicate isn't an art you're born with but a skill you learn.

How we were brought up affects the way we can and do relate to our partners, in several important ways. The way our parents behaved to us and to each other serves as a model for how we behave with our partners. It is in our own childhood that we first learn what we should expect from a relationship and from ourselves and our partners as a couple. From our parents we pick up our ideas of who makes decisions in and outside the home, who earns the money, who manages the budget, who does the housework. But it's not just the nuts and bolts of how we run a relationship, and expect each other to act as a couple, that we copy from them. We also have demonstrated to us how partners relate to each other, and we see emotions either made legitimate and acceptable, or made taboo. We may learn that sex is not something you talk about and affection is not something you show. We may learn that voices are never raised and anger never shown, or that throwing cups, cushions and punches is the way to react when you're upset. If we grow up feeling that our childhood experiences could be improved upon and that our adult relationships will heal all wounds, we may find this hard to put into action. Most of us have a good idea of what we did like and what we didn't like, how we would and how we wouldn't want to be. But at the same time few of us have a reliable blueprint for knowing how to do it differently from the way we were brought up ourselves. Our own parents are our role models and even if we don't like what they did, we find ourselves falling into and following the patterns they set and taught us by example.

Our own experiences of what passes for communication may not have been beneficial, and may not have left us with positive feelings about talking and sharing. Can you remember any proverbs or old sayings that encourage you to talk and share your thoughts, feelings and worries with other people? For example:

- A problem shared is a problem halved.

Most well-known phrases and sayings emphasise exactly the opposite:

- Laugh and the world laughs with you. Cry and you cry alone.
- Least said soonest mended.
- Those that ask don't get.
- Silence is golden.
- What you don't know, can't hurt you.

Can you remember any more, and were there any that were particularly quoted in your family? Discuss with your partner how this may have affected you. Did it make it easy or hard for you to open up to other people, especially your partner?

Listening

'Listen to what the other person is saying' may sound obvious advice, but we often don't follow it. How many times have you had a so-called conversation with another person and realised from the beginning that they weren't listening to a word you said? How often do you talk to someone, and know that they're simply waiting for a gap in your words to jump in with their pre-prepared speech? And how often have you talked with someone and simply not known whether they were listening or interested, because their attention appeared to be elsewhere? It's more than a little off-putting to be trying to open your heart to someone whose eyes are glazed over or looking at something or someone else. We do it ourselves, too. How often, two minutes after you've finished talking with a friend or your partner, would you be able to repeat what they'd said to you, even vaguely? You may love someone, share a life and a bed with them and have years of being together. But the fact remains that if you want to understand what they think and feel, why they do certain things and how to get on the same wavelength, you have to enlist their point of view. And if you want to make it clear that you are attending, you need to know how.

It's actually very easy – depressingly easy – to stop someone from opening up to you. You may pride yourself on being a good listener, you may want to be available and sympathetic, but how often do we interrupt, impose our own ideas, finish sentences, switch off, talk too much or contradict the other person when they're trying to communicate? We may feel, while doing all these things, that we're showing how much we're in tune. From the other person's point of view, we may be doing nothing of the sort. Have a look at these dialogues between Efia and her husband Kofi, who have both just got home from work.

'Hi, Efia. Had a good day?'
'Well, not really. I've been thinking about . . .'
'Come on, cheer up, it may never happen.'
'Well, I think it already has. That phone bill we got . . .'

'Oh, you don't want to worry about that. I'll do a bit of overtime and it'll all be sorted.'

'Kofi, that's not the point . . .'

'You shouldn't take things so seriously.'

The reason I'm on the phone all the time is . . .'

'It's just a phone bill, it's not the end of the world.'

'Oh, forget it!'

'Hey, was there something you wanted to say to me?'

'Hi, Efia. Had a good day?'

'Well, not really. We got the phone bill today.'

'Yeah, I saw it. It's twice as much as last time and none of those damn calls are mine.'

'I know and I think we have to talk ...'

'Don't you think you've done enough talking for a bit? You're always nattering away to someone or other and I'm sick of it.'

'Well it's not all my fault.'

'Oh, whose bloody fault is it? Mine, I suppose.'

'Well, in a way, yes it is.'

'Yeah, blame me it's always down to me. Sometimes I wonder why on earth you stay with me.'

'And at times like this, I wonder the same!'

'Hi, Efia. Had a good day?'

'Well, not really. The phone . . .'

'Did you ring your mother back? She called the other day.'

'Yes, but I wanted to talk to you . . .'

'Dunno what you two find to talk about all the time, I really don't.'

'Well that's sort of what I wanted . . .'

'Hey, that film is on tomorrow, want to go?'

'No, I wanted to look at the bill with . . .'

'It's all right, I'll pay it next week, don't worry about it.'

'Yes, but Kofi, we need . . .'

'To get tea on the table, I know. I'll go peel the potatoes.'

(Sighs and gives up)

'Hi, Efia. Had a good day?'

'Well, not really. The phone bill came in and it's really high this quarter.'

'Hmmm? Yes, sure, I've been paying all my petrol on card this year.'

'No, not the credit card bill, the phone bill.'

(Grunts)

'I've been spending a lot of time on the phone and I want to talk to you about it. Hey, Kofi?'

'Yeah, yeah. Hey, they're showing the Grand Prix tonight. Can't wait!'

'Kofi!'

'What? Want a coffee? I'll just turn the TV on while the kettle boils. What were you saying?'

'Never mind.'

'Hi Efia. Had a good day?'

'Well, not really. The phone bill came in and it's higher than it was last quarter.'

'Nah, I'm sure it's not.'

'Yes it is. And we need to talk about why . . .'

'There's nothing to worry about, you've made a mistake, or they have. Forget it.'

'But Kofi, we need to discuss this!'

'There's nothing to discuss. You've got it wrong, I'm sure.'

In all these examples, the way Kofi responded put up barriers to Efia confiding in him or getting what she wanted and needed from the conversation. Each time, he stopped Efia dead in her tracks by interrupting, imposing his ideas, finishing sentences, switching off, talking too much or contradicting. He might have wanted to be helpful or sympathetic, or he might not have wanted to hear what she was trying to tell him. Whatever, they failed to connect.

Think about the people you might know or have seen on television who you would say are 'good listeners'. What is it that they do to make you feel comfortable and able to confide in them, and get what you need from the exchange? There is a skill to listening in a way that opens people up instead of shutting them up; it's called active listening. It's not instinctive, it's a learned skill. You can acquire it, and here's how.

Think of being able to communicate as an ability similar to riding a bike or swimming. You start off as a beginner, needing to pick up the basics. Once you understand how it's done, you have to practise to become expert and confident. To be a good communicator you need to know how to listen, and just as importantly, how to let the other person know you're listening. You also have to be in touch with your own emotions, be honest about where you're coming from, and able to accept both your own and the other person's feelings.

The first step is learning how to listen.

I talk, you talk

This will help you learn how to hear when your partner wants to talk to you, and how to talk so they will hear you. It's a game that gives you both tasks you have to complete. Sit facing each other and agree that each of you should take a turn being the listener and the speaker. Use a kitchen timer or alarm clock to mark time – you can start with two minutes each. During this two minutes, the speaker should talk, on any subject they choose. They have to keep on talking for that time. While they're doing that, the listener's task is to hear and encourage them to talk – but without saying a single word. The listener isn't allowed to interrupt, ask questions or make comments. What they should do is help the speaker along with nods and the sort of 'Uh-huh', 'Um' and 'Ah?' sounds that say 'Yes, go on, I'm hearing you'.

You may like to try this a few times. After the first attempt, talk over with your companion how it felt. How did it feel just to listen and not ask questions? How did it feel to be listened to, knowing you wouldn't be interrupted in any way? Both are a lot harder than you think, mainly because we're not used to doing either. Interrupting, asking questions, finishing sentences don't help communication. We often do them either to show off or to take control of the situation. Or, we do it to stop the other person saying something we don't want to hear. Even if we do want to listen, we often find it hard to let the other person have space to make their feelings clear because we're not used to standing back and listening. But making it clear you are listening and taking in what the other person is saying can be reassuring and empowering. Being heard gives the speaker a chance to hear themselves, too. Instead of wasting energy on making you pay attention, bringing the subject back to what they wanted to discuss or arguing with you, you can soon understand each other. It often feels very awkward and odd at first, on both sides. You'll get used to it, and be amazed at how effective it is as a tool.

Once you've tried active listening, go one stage further and add reflective listening to your skills.

Reflective listening

Again, you each have a job to do. Sit facing each other and agree that each of you should take a turn being the listener and the speaker. Use a kitchen timer or alarm clock to mark time – you can start with two minutes each. The speaker gets two minutes to talk, on any subject they choose. Their only task is to keep talking. The listener's task is to show they're both listening and understanding what is being said. They do this by echoing back to the speaker what has been said. So, this time, instead of saying 'Uh-huh' or 'Um' to what they say, you restate what they've said. You can use their words or your own words. Reflective listening isn't just parroting, it's rephrasing and checking out. Which means you don't have to get it entirely right first time, every time – the speaker will correct you and it still works. What you are trying to do is to listen and hear what they are saying, not putting your words into their mouth. It will sound a lot stranger to the person doing the reflective listening than to the speaker. Useful phrases to

---

use in front of your mirrored speech may be: 'It sounds as if you're saying . . .'; 'I imagine you're feeling . . .'; 'It seems to me that what you're saying is . . .'; 'What I hear you saying is . . .'; 'So, you're saying . . .'; 'So, let me get this right . . .'; 'If I can just check this out . . .'.

You may like to try this a few times. After the first attempt, talk over with your companion how it felt. How did it feel to be focusing on the other person's words in order to be able to repeat them back accurately? How did it feel to have the other person repeating your words back at you? Having your own words coming back at you not only gives you the chance to hear what you've said and clarify it, but makes you fully reassured that you have been understood.

You can see how Kofi got on with Efia when he tried using these skills.

'Hi, Efia. Had a good day?'

'Well, not really. The phone bill came in and it's higher than it was last quarter.'

'Uh-huh?'

'Yes. I'm really worried about it.'

'Ummm?'

'Look, Kofi, it's not the money that's got me worried, it's what it means.'

'You're worried because the phone bill is higher than it was last quarter?'

'No, I'm worried because it's higher because I spend most evenings on the phone.'

'It seems to me you're really upset about this.'

'Yes, I'm upset because I don't feel we've been talking much and that's why I've been talking to other people.'

'We haven't been talking lately.'

'That's right. And I think I know why and what it's about but every time I try to talk to you, you don't seem to be listening.'

'Well, I'm listening now.'

In this last example, Kofi used another helpful technique, which is giving feelings a name. When Efia said 'No, I'm worried because it's higher because I spend most evenings on the phone', he thought about what her emotions might be, and put a name to them by responding 'I can see you feel upset about this'. If he'd been wrong, and she was angry or guilty or confused, by that stage in the conversation the chances are that she would have corrected him without breaking the flow, and gone on. When you have the tone right in an exchange, you can check out what might be being said without it seeming that you're misunderstanding.

Giving feelings a name

Giving feelings a name is an important part of valuing and validating what people feel, and what they are. Arguments or lack of understanding come about between people so often because we don't accept what the other is saying.

'I've had an awful day!'
'It can't be all that bad.'

'I hate that bloody man!'
'Hey, steady on, that's a bit strong.'

'I'm starving!'
'Don't talk daft, I've just seen you demolish a packet of biscuits.'

'I'm so depressed I could just sit down and cry!'
'Cheer up, it'll never happen.'

'It's not fair!'
'Have a cup of tea and it'll be better.'

'Nobody ever listens to me!'
'Don't be stupid, I heard every bloody word.'

'Everything I do goes wrong!'

'You're being silly.'

Denying feelings

We often deny another person's feelings because what they are saying is something we don't want to hear. When you deny a feeling it doesn't go away, but the person expressing that emotion is left with a triple load. They still have the uncomfortable emotion, because even though they've tried to offload on to you and thus deal with it, you've shoved it back into their arms. They also have the added emotional burden of anger, hurt or bafflement (or all three) with you for not hearing. Worst of all, they're left confused and distrusting their own feelings. They've clearly announced their emotional state to you, and you've said it doesn't exist. If that happens often enough in your life you start to doubt your own responses.

The reason we do this is not necessarily because we don't believe our partner is going through these difficulties. Sometimes, our motive is that we believe that if we can argue away the feelings, deny their very existence, we can banish them. We feel we are helping our partner best by trying to make the anger, pain or confusion go away. That's why, when someone bursts into tears, we often say 'There, there, it's all right', when clearly it isn't all right! We leap to make it better in the way we have been taught – by arguing over the existence of the bad feeling. It's as if we feel that if we deny the existence of this negative emotion it will vanish into thin air. We fear acknowledging it will give it substance and make it live.

We also do this because we see our partner's response as a comment on and criticism of ourselves. If our partner feels bad, we assume we are failing them. We also feel uncomfortable in admitting to the reality of unhappy emotions as if recognising them makes them our fault.

None of this works, of course. The truth is that bad feelings exist whether we like them or not, or whether we accept and acknowledge them or not. You're not going to patch up a disagreement with your partner by burying your head in the sand and refusing to see that they're angry, miserable, hurt or upset. All you'll do is prolong the problem. By giving feelings a name, you soon find that allowing bad feelings is the first step in learning to handle them and to let go of them.

Acknowledging emotions

Good listening is about allowing the other person an opinion, not totally agreeing with it or surrendering your own. You can listen, and accept that this is how they might be feeling or seeing a situation, without condoning what they think or saying you see it the same way. In fact, sometimes being a 'Yes person' and agreeing with everything they say prevents the other person from progressing. Side with your partner as they protest that the boss has been unfair or a shop assistant was rude, and you prevent them from working through their emotions to accept that they might have contributed to the difficulty and need to compromise. But by acknowledging their emotions and accepting that they exist, you tell them that their feelings are acceptable and that they as people are valued by you. Everyone is entitled to be angry sometimes, and entitled to have conflicting feelings, too.

'I've had an awful day!'
'It sounds as if you've had a rough time today.'

'I hate that bloody man!'
'You sound pretty angry at him. Want to tell me about it?'

'I'm so depressed I could just sit down and cry!'
'You're feeling really sad at the moment.'

'It's not fair!'
'You're feeling as if people are being unfair.'

'Nobody ever listens to me!'
'You don't feel as if people are listening to you.'

'Everything I do goes wrong!'
'You're feeling as if you can't do anything right.'

One major problem in many people's lives is that they waste far too much time and effort denying angry and negative feelings. How often have you tried to pretend to yourself and everyone else that you don't feel angry, hurt, miserable, envious or scared? How many times have you said 'I'm fine, nothing's wrong!' when what you really wanted to scream was 'I feel TERRIBLE!' and be given a hug. We're scared of negative feelings because we fear they will overwhelm us and get out of control. But reflecting and allowing feelings doesn't prolong them or enlarge them or make them real where otherwise they would not have existed or come out. Acknowledging feelings allows them to be discharged. Even temper tantrums are actually very healthy – a good shout, moan or sob gets it all out of the system.

Are you fine?

The next time someone asks you how you feel and you say 'Fine', reflect on this alternative definition for that word. It can mean 'OK'. It can also mean

F   ucked up
I   nsecure
N   eurotic
E   motionally unstable

Which usually describes it just about perfectly, doesn't it?

Accepting feelings

Accept a person's feelings and you will find several advantages flow from this. You may both discover more about the situation than you originally realised.

'You're a total b*****d, Syed, I'm so mad at you! You left me with an empty tank and I nearly ran out of petrol!'

'You sound really angry with me.'

'Yes, I am. I just drove all the way back from my mother's with one eye on the gauge. Everything's closed and I thought I was going to get stuck.'

'I can hear you're furious and I'm sorry.'

'Well, to tell you the truth I was more scared. I was terrified the car would stall and I'd be out there, alone.'

'You were scared of being alone.'

'Well, come to think of it, I was upset even before I noticed the petrol gauge. Mum wasn't looking too well. It sort of frightened me but you know what she's like, she won't complain or ask for help. I was working myself up into a state and then I thought I was going to be stuck on the roadside.'

'It sounds as if you'd like a bit of support next time you go and see her. Shall I come along so you won't be alone?'

'Hey, I'd really like that!'

Listening to your partner doesn't mean that you lose the argument or your own position. That's really what's behind most of our difficulties in taking someone else's point of view on board. We think that if we hear them, their ideas will overwhelm ours and we'll lose out. We also fear that just accepting the feelings will allow emotion to run riot and sense to be lost. Neither is true. By listening to what the other person is saying you set up a situation where both of you can hear each other. From that, you can negotiate and compromise. By accepting what your partner feels, you underline that you trust them, hear them and accept them and their feelings.

'Oh, for God's sake, Jane!'

'I can hear you feel really angry with me.'

'You've b***** gone and done it again!'

'You're really mad at me, aren't you?'

'Yes, I am.'

'Can you tell me what you're angry about?'

'You've gone and asked Pete and Sue over for a meal and you never asked me if that was OK with me.'

'Yeah, you're right. I should have cleared it with you first. I really like Sue and wanted to see them both again. But I should have asked you first. Can we leave it as it is this time but I really will talk to you first before making any other arrangements?'

Part of the wish to deny feelings is the fear that we can't do anything about them. Most of us simply hate feeling helpless. You may be surprised to find that, sometimes, just acknowledging an emotion does the trick and gets rid of it.

'I've had an awful day!'

'You feel you've had a bad time today.'

'I made a stupid mistake at work and had to spend hours clearing it up. When I went for lunch I'd left half my money at home and had to make do without a coffee. And to cap it all, I got caught in a thunderstorm – I'm soaked!'

'You feel pretty fed up, no wonder.'

'Too right I do. Anyway, thanks for being sympathetic! Give us a kiss, and tell me what's for supper?'

'I' messages

Many of the circular arguments in which we find ourselves stuck are due to the 'You', 'We' and 'Everyone' messages we tend to use. Think back to the last argument you had. What did you say to your partner? Was it something along these lines?

'You never listen to a word I say!'

'You're so selfish.'

'We don't think that's a very good idea.'

'Everybody says you're making a fool of yourself.'

Each statement has one thing in common: they put the responsibility for what is being done or said on another person. Each is a
label and an accusation. 'You' messages tell the person you're talking
to that it's all their fault. 'We' messages say that you're not the only
one who thinks this, you have back-up and support in your accusa-
tions. And 'Everyone' messages say your accusation is none of your
doing, you're just passing on the majority view.

'You', 'We' and 'Everyone' messages all demand the person you're
talking to should change to do something the way you want. Most
of all, each statement says you don't like them for being like that.
None of these statements gives a proper account of why you are
objecting. They don't suggest a constructive solution. They don't
allow for discussion. And, worst of all, they often say you know the
other person can't change because that's the way they are. 'You',
'We' and 'Everyone' messages seldom make the person being
accused sit up, smile sweetly and say, 'Hey, I see what you mean!
You're right, I'll do it different!' They usually make the other person
feel angry, defensive, useless, humiliated and/or hurt. And, of
course, ready to strike back and have a row.

The opposite of a 'You', 'We' or 'Everyone' message is an 'I'
message. 'I' messages make it very clear that you, the person
speaking, are the one who feels this way – not the crowd, your
mother or your friends. 'I' messages are also about your own feelings
about what is happening, not about what the other person is doing.
Instead of saying 'You never listen to a word I say', an 'I' message
might be, 'I feel upset when you don't appear to have heard what
I've said.' Instead of blaming or being judgmental, an 'I' message
puts across your feelings and says how and why you feel the other
person's actions have contributed to this. But you are not saying
that they meant to do it this way. You are asking them to think
about how you feel, and inviting them to talk about it. 'I' messages
take responsibility for what you are feeling and saying instead of
trying to hide behind or blame other people. When you use strong
'I' messages you can be pleasantly surprised by having the other
person say 'Oh, I really didn't know you felt like this. Can we come
to an agreement?'

The key phrase for using 'I' messages is 'I feel . . .'. But to use it so that it makes sense, and really works, you do have to be genuine. It's no good just slapping 'I feel' on the beginning of a question, statement or complaint: 'I feel you're being a pain-in-the-butt' is a 'You', 'We' and 'Everyone' message in very poor disguise! To use 'I feel' messages effectively, you really do need to confront your own emotions and come clean about how you are reacting and what you are feeling about the situation.

Look at these 'You' messages: Can you turn them into 'I' messages? Add some of your own.

> ### Example
> 'You' message: 'What's the matter with you? I've asked you ten times to take out the rubbish and now I've had to do it – again. You're so selfish.'
> 'I' message: 'I feel annoyed when I ask you to do something and it doesn't get done.'

'You' message: 'You never listen to a thing I say!'
'I' message:

'You' message: 'You never take me out anymore.'
'I' message:

'You' message: 'Now look what you've made me do! Tea's ruined and it's all your fault.'
'I' message:

'We' message: 'It's not my fault I'm late, we were so busy today.'
'I' message:

'Everyone' message: 'You look terrible in that, everyone thinks so.'
'I' message:

Of course, 'I' messages only work if you really are expressing your feelings. We have difficulties expressing feelings in our culture, mainly because, not being used to doing so, we often can't even put a name to our own feelings. Reasoning – that is, trying to find a solution to disagreements through talking – doesn't mean you always have to be reasonable. Feelings are very rarely open to cold logic and if you are trying to reach an agreement and understanding over something that strikes an emotional chord, but trying to do it in an unemotional way, the message will be mixed and therefore dishonest.

Della found herself getting upset whenever her partner Dane tidied up around her. They had endless arguments over this, usually beginning like this:

'Dane, you're driving me crazy! I put the news section of the Sunday papers on the sofa because I'd read it. You've put it back on the pile, all neat and tidy. Do you have to do that? And while we're about it, you put the T-shirt I left on the bed in the wash when I hadn't finished with it. And stop washing up whatever cooking implement I'm using whenever we cook. I keep trying to stir the spaghetti and find you've washed up and put the bloody spoon away, again!'

'Well, don't leave the place in such a mess then.'

'I don't! You're just such a neurotic Mr Clean you'd drive anyone to drink!'

Having learnt about 'I' messages, she started to use them:

'Dane, will you please not tidy up the papers until I've finished reading them. It really upsets me.'

'Well, don't make such a mess of them then.'

Della realised that she still wasn't actually sending an 'I' message. So she dug deep into her own feelings to find the genuine emotion she had when Dane tidied up around her. She realised that, like many of us, she wasn't exactly sure at first what emotion she had been experiencing. Difficulties in communication often come about because we say one thing and mean another. How can your partner take your irritation about tidying up newspapers seriously when, deep down, he or she knows only too well that this isn't the reason for your outburst. And how can you sort out your misunderstandings unless you can identify what you really do feel? To get in touch with her feelings, Della used a feelings exercise.

Feelings exercise

Do this exercise with your partner or a close friend. Most of us find it hard, and often frightening, to get in touch with emotions. That doesn't only apply to the painful emotions such as fear or anger. It also means that we sometimes hold love, happiness and joy at bay. After all, once we let the barriers down to one we may be overwhelmed by all of them. Doing this exercise may be surprisingly powerful, so do it when you feel safe and secure, with someone you care about and trust.

Have a look at this list of emotions. How many of them strike a chord with you? Are they feelings from the present or the past? Are there any you feel, but call by another name? Are there some you find too scary to be comfortable in feeling?

joyful	stressed	cold	pleased	incompetent
calm	lustful	grieved	bored	foolish
loved	panicked	worried	happy	inadequate
loving	warm	despairing	contemptuous	satisfied
miserable	peaceful	disgusted	sympathetic	amused
angry	elated	uneasy	hatred	confident
despairing	silly	confused	trapped	relaxed
hesitant	proud	cheated	jealous	envious
hopeful	stubborn	hesitant	lost	embarrassed
serious	serene	offended	indifferent	abandoned
excited	impudent	exuberant	merry	anxious
lonely	stupid	eager	listless	enthusiastic

Are there any others you'd like to add to the list?

The two questions you should always ask yourself when looking at emotions are:

- What am I feeling?
- When have I felt like this before?

Asking the second sometimes helps you work out the real answer to the first question. This is because one of the main barriers that could come between you and your partner is often unfinished business from your childhood, which can have a powerful effect on your relationship. If your parents behaved towards you in ways that you found confusing, unsatisfying, painful or frightening, it can have effects on the way we are able to love and trust. It also, most importantly, has profound effects on the way we feel we deserve to love and be loved.

When Della did a feelings exercise, she realised her emotion wasn't upset, it was feelings of loss and of being devalued. And when she asked herself when she had felt like this before, she found herself thinking of her childhood and her father. Her father had always, she felt, been on at her to clear up her toys, her books, her clothes. He had worked at home so even the family rooms, such as the living-room and kitchen, were considered by him to be public areas that should be kept neat. Della could remember feeling positively panicked about keeping her belongings out of the way. And when she really thought about it she realised that she felt as if her home was not her own. She felt she had to clear up all evidence of her very existence, as if her father was ashamed of her or didn't value her. So, next time, she tried this:

'Dane, my Dad was always on at me to tidy up and I think that's why I hate it when you do it.'

'For heaven's sake, Della, you're a 40-year-old woman not a 10-year-old and I'm certainly not your Dad!'

Della needed the final step in getting feelings across, which is to be open, honest and clear. She needed to match the outward message to the inward feeling, and not send a mixed message. Even when we get round to identifying what we really feel, we don't always make this clear to the person we're talking to. Either we want to be polite, or we don't want to scare the person with our feelings, or we're embarrassed about the way we feel. Think of the way you sometimes laugh or giggle when in fact you are angry or frightened. Think of the way you make a joke about your feelings or accept them being minimised or made trivial, when you actually feel strongly. Della realised her emotional reaction had been so strong that she had been trying to hide it. She felt pain and loss, but it came out as mild reproof. A good formula to use when you want to be clear is: 'When you (*do so-and-so*) I feel (*this emotion*) because (*this is the reason I feel it*) so please (*this is what I would like you to do*).' And as you say it, let the emotion show!

'Dane, when you tidy up I feel so unloved and devalued. I remember when my Dad used to do it at home and I felt as if I wasn't supposed to be there, that all my belongings were a mess that shouldn't be seen. It makes me feel so unwanted. Could you please let the papers lie until the end of the evening?'

'Della, I had no idea it upset you as much as that. Listen, let's see if we can work something out that suits us both. I hate mess but I'm sure we can agree a compromise.'

Putting all these skills together, you can now look at what happens when Leona and Wayne use communication skills to find out what is really happening in their brewing argument, beginning with Leona not assuming the worst about Wayne's behaviour.

	What they said	**How it came over**	**What s/he was thinking**	**What s/he really felt**
Leona	Let's go out tonight, Wayne.	No time to sit around, let's go, let's go!	I've had a hard week and I really could do with a treat.	Tired, fed up.
Wayne	Do we have to?	Yo, man, all I want to do is veg out.	Hey, come on – I'd rather spend time at home with you.	In need of quality time.
Leona	I've had a really hard day. I just feel in need of a bit of a treat.	Up-front and honest.	I've gone off on the wrong foot, let's make myself clear.	Concerned.
Wayne	And going out is a treat?	Hurt.	That's not very loving.	Offended.
Leona	You sound a bit down.	Tell me about it.	Whoops – he's upset. I've said the wrong thing so I'd better find out what's wrong.	Ready to listen.
Wayne	No, I'm fine.	Don't touch.	Please try a bit harder.	Yes, I'm down.
Leona	Let me sit here with you for a bit.	I'll wait.	Give him a moment and he'll come across.	Supportive.
Wayne	Actually, I'm not feeling so hot.	Grudging admission.	Oh, all right then.	I HURT.
Leona	You're not feeling very happy?	Concerned.	Ok, I'm not laughing, he does sound down.	Sympathetic.
Wayne	Well, it seems you spend more time talking with other people than me.	I know, I'm whingeing.	I really want her to hear this.	Plaintive.

	What they said	**How it came over**	**What s/he was thinking**	**What s/he really felt**
Leona	You think I talk to other people more than you?	Listening.	I didn't realise he felt like that.	Taken aback.
Wayne	Well, when we were in the pub on Sunday night you seemed happier to be with your girl friends.	Hurt.	And I felt neglected.	I've been wanting to say this all week.
Leona	You sound fed up about that.	I see what you were upset about.	So that was what this is all about.	Aha!
Wayne	Wouldn't you be?	Loosening up a bit.	At least she's listening.	Heard.
Leona	You're feeling hurt because you think I'd rather spend time with other people and that's why you don't want to go out tonight.	Checking it out.	Let's get this totally clear.	Relieved – we can work this out.
Wayne	When you put it like that it sounds stupid. But, yes, that's what I felt.	Abashed.	She'll laugh at me.	Embarrassed.

	What they said	How it came over	What s/he was thinking	What s/he really felt
Leona	I want to spend time, alone, with you too. I just didn't want to cook or do any washing-up tonight and I thought I'd give us both a treat and we'd go out. I'm really sorry you thought I was ignoring you. In fact, I thought you wanted to be with your mates and I was giving you some slack. So we both had the wrong end of the stick.	Straight, honest, putting her feelings on the line.	Let's see if we can get this cleared up.	Loving.
Wayne	Oh, I see. Hey, let's compromise. What about we stay in and get a takeaway?	Willing to negotiate.	She does love me!	Whoopee!
Leona	Ace!	Happy.	What a relief – I thought he'd gone off me!	Happy.

Strokes

Sometimes we forget how much we need to value others, and to be valued by them. We all need to be complimented and thanked and appreciated. Often, we forget how easy it is to give pleasure and how a little would mean a lot. The sort of action that gives a lift to morale is called 'a stroke'. Strokes can be spoken – telling someone you love them, thanking them for helping you or saying you value them. Don't ever assume that you don't need to say it. The answer to the question 'Do you love me?' isn't 'Well, we're together, aren't we?' It isn't 'Hang on a second I'm watching the news'. It isn't 'Don't bother me now I've got a headache'. It isn't 'How can I think about love while the cat's being sick and the kids are running riot?' And it isn't 'Love? It all depends what you mean by love.' The answer is yes. YES. YES. Make a point of telling your partner, unasked, that you love them at the very minimum of once a day. Once an hour is preferable. But showing it by your actions can be just as important too. You can show it by contact – hugging or kissing someone or giving them a back rub. Or you can act out your feelings – making them a cup of coffee, giving them a small present or doing a chore you know they'd like done.

Try these strokes, or think of some of your own:

- Make your partner an unexpected tea or coffee and tell them you just thought they might like it.

- Ask your partner what they would like to do this weekend if they really had a free choice and, budget permitting, pull out all the stops on something that fits the bill.

- Keep your eyes and ears open for something you know would hit the spot as an 'un-birthday present'. If your partner has a particular interest or hobby, for instance, you might find a book or a video on the subject. It doesn't have to cost much – it really is the thought that counts.

- Offer to pamper your partner by giving them a foot rub or massage, run a hot bath and leave them in peace with a drink, or be on hand to scrub their back.

- Change into something special for the evening and when they ask what's the occasion, say 'Being with you'.

- Make a list of strokes you'd like to give and a list of strokes you'd like to receive. Ask your partner to do the same. Discuss your lists and agree to give each other at least one stroke a day.

It is common and understandable for us to lose the honeymoon feeling when a relationship lasts. Once the early days are over, you can find yourself mislaying the first rush of emotions and prey to unhelpful expectations that stop you developing something better to put in their place. Instead of discussions, you start to have arguments that often go nowhere. In the next section, we'll look at how to turn disagreements to your advantage and make them a way of getting back the sparkle and enjoyment of your first love affair.

3

How to Have a Good Row

All healthy relationships have conflict – it's how you argue that can make the difference between a dynamic and loving partnership and one that hurts. That you quarrel is not the problem; it's how you argue and whether you end your arguments that matter. Conflict is destructive to a relationship in two main circumstances. The first is when you make use of intimate secrets and trust to wound the other during a fight. The second is when you never actually put arguments to rest, but let them simmer on, returning to them again and again. Frequently, this is because neither of you is bringing the true point of conflict into the open. What you're shouting about is not what you're in reality upset or angry about. This makes it impossible for either of you to understand what the real argument is about, or to ever settle the matter. If you want a relationship that will stand up, you need to be prepared to cope with disagreement, for you and your partner to share thoughts and feelings and have a good understanding. You can't read minds, so when you don't know what the other thinks, you should ask, and when you're not sure the other knows how you feel, you should tell them. A healthy and happy relationship is one in which you both know how to get what you want without treading on each other's toes or putting each other down. In order to achieve this, to let that honeymoon feeling last, you need to know how to have a good row, turning an argument into a discussion. It's totally unrealistic to expect to get rid of rows from your relationship. What you can do is make arguments less painful and the effects helpful rather than destructive.

We tend to argue for a variety of reasons. The obvious one may seem to be that you have a difference of opinion and don't feel the other person is hearing or taking notice of what you are saying. But arguments are like icebergs: at least nine-tenths are under the surface. Most arguments have very little to do with the here and now: whether you paint the bathroom blue or green, which in-laws you spend the next festival with or whose fault it is that the credit card bill's too high. When you fight, not only do you frequently bring in grudges from the past ('And another thing, you always . . .') but your past histories run the argument for you, like a ghostly film script that puts words in your mouth and emotions in your heart.

One way the past affects our arguments is a question of style. When there is friction, the way we deal with it has a lot to do with how we've grown up seeing how rows develop and are resolved – or not – in our families of origin. In some families, raised voices or wounding comments are the way those around us communicated with anyone they loved, so this is how we learn to do it. In others, open conflict is something we saw avoided. Instead, battles were fought slyly and in a round-about fashion, with subjects skated around but never approached head-on. The message you might have taken from your early days was that facing up squarely to emotions and sharing your thoughts makes you vulnerable and leads to disaster, so you avoid it at all costs. Another style is denial, where partners simply refuse to acknowledge there's even a problem. In other relationships, partners may be quick to shift the blame. You think problems are always something's or someone's fault, and you don't want it to be yours. In all these situations, arguments tend to last and be very difficult to resolve.

Do you talk?

Do you talk – really talk – to your partner? How good are you at communicating? Not about whether he wants fish fingers or steak for supper, or you want to go out or stay in tonight, but about whether you're feeling fed up or happy, sexy or playful. Being in tune, physically and emotionally, with the person you love is not about knowing exactly what the other is thinking. That's an unrealistic fantasy because we'd need to be mind-readers to do that. But couples who talk to each other have the next best thing, the ability to ask and the willingness to listen to each other. Sometimes we avoid the issue, deny there's anything wrong if we're upset or blame our partner for our own ills. Sometimes, instead of communicating, what we do is row – endlessly and fruitlessly. Try this quiz to see how you and your partner often interact:

How do you and your partner communicate?
You've had a terrible day, and your partner comes in with a face like thunder. Do you:

1 Do the washing-up, with as much banging and clattering as possible?
2 When s/he asks 'What's up?' say 'Nothing'?
3 Make a cup of tea, say 'I'm feeling awful. You've had a bad day too. Let's take turns spilling it out'?
4 Ask your partner why they can't come home with a smile on their face for once?

A row is brewing. Do you:

1 Make yourself scarce?
2 Blithely carry on as if nothing is happening?
3 Tell your partner what is bothering you and ask them how they see it?
4 Accuse your partner of picking an argument?

Uncle Joe has died leaving you £4,000. One of you wants a new kitchen, the other wants to blow it all on the holiday of a lifetime. Do you:

1 Tiptoe round the subject until summer is halfway over?
2 Tell your partner you don't care, it's their decision?
3 Sit down and thrash out the pros and cons of each choice?
4 Make your partner's life hell with complaints about the washing machine?

It's your birthday and the one thing you really want is to be taken out for a meal. Does your partner:

1 Forget what day it is?
2 Give you a set of pans as your present and expect you to cook dinner?
3 Ask you a week before what you'd like, and surprise you on the night?
4 Take you to their favourite event and swear it's what they thought you'd like?

You're making love and you know that if your partner does *this*, it'll really light your fire, but if they do *that* it won't. Do you:

1 Heave a secret sigh and hope for the best?

2 Tell yourself it doesn't matter, you're not really bothered?

3 Say 'Hey, it really feels good when you touch me here, like this'?

4 Think 'They ought to know how to do it for me', and sulk when they don't?

You can't remember when you last made love. Do you:

1 Paint the bathroom?

2 Try not to think about it?

3 Say 'We've been ignoring each other for far too long – how about making love tonight?'

4 Wear your best and slap on the cologne in the hope that looking good might spark their interest?

Your partner wants to try something new in bed. Do they:

1 Have sexual fantasies about it?

2 Tell themselves that sort of stuff is perverted?

3 Say 'We've never tried swinging from the chandelier and it sounds fun. Shall we?'

4 Complain to friends what a stick-in-the-mud you are?

You have a sex problem. Do you:

1 Ignore it – it will go away in time?

2 Tell yourself everyone loses interest at your time in life?

3 Cuddle up to your partner in bed, ask to talk and suggest you both see your GP for a chat and check up?

4 Go on a diet because you know the problem is that your partner doesn't fancy you?

What do your answers suggest about your style of communication with each other? There are no 'wrong' or 'right' answers

– but answering mostly 1s would suggest you avoid confronting difficulties. Answering mostly 2s would suggest you deny there is a problem or your feelings about it. Answering mostly 3s would suggest that you and your partner do talk things over. And answering mostly 4s would suggest that you look for someone to blame because you usually think it's your own fault.

Arguing

How you argue has a lot to do with your upbringing and childhood. When you argue may have much to do with events in your life at the time, and how they relate to your past. When we're under stress, we often find ourselves going back to childish behaviour. The stress can be at work, in the family or in our intimate relationship. If you find your relationship coming under increased strain, the two questions you should ask are:

- What has changed?
- When have I felt like this before?

Arguments tend to surface or increase when the balance of a relationship in some way alters.

Julie and David went to counselling for help when they realised that they were arguing every day. Says Julie: 'We always bickered a lot but then it got serious. We used to have happy periods with the odd bicker and then it became one long quarrel with only the odd flash of happiness.' When they looked at their relationship, they gradually recognised that it took a turn for the worse when Julie had a pregnancy scare. 'My period was late and we were both relieved when it came, because having a child at that point wasn't in the game plan. But gradually, after that, our arguments got a lot more nasty.' What had changed had been that both of them had had to think about their 'sensible' decision to leave starting a family until later. What Julie felt unable to admit to herself, let alone David, was that she really would have been delighted to have become pregnant. Because they hadn't talked it over out loud, she didn't realise that David felt the same. Unspoken resentment created a barrier between them. In addition, both had feelings of rejection and loss, harking back for Julie to the time her mother had a miscarriage and the whole family mourned a baby that never was. And for David, it brought back memories of his first girlfriend, who became pregnant and under pressure from her mother, had an abortion and finished their relationship.

Who you argue with has everything to do with the depth and strength of your relationships. In a way, you pay a backhand compliment to anyone with whom you fight. We don't fight with people to whom we are indifferent. When it comes to family and friends, our bitterest rows may well be with the ones who mean the most to us. It's very easy to find ourselves lashing out at the people we love, especially the person with whom we're most intimate. Partly that's because we trust them enough to take our negative feelings head on and still love us. But being close and intimate with someone also means they know enough about us to hurt when they want. It also means we make ourselves open and vulnerable so that, without meaning it, our partner may touch a raw nerve and we react. But how often has that nerve been made raw by someone or something way outside our own, present four walls? Arguments very often arise because of the hidden nine-tenths, those parts of our lives and our pasts that have little to do with the actual person we're screaming at. You may find yourself taking out your anger, fear or pain on your partner when it's someone or something else entirely who touched you off. When partners clash, it's often a case of 'Kicking the cat', 'Transferring a legacy' or 'Passing the buck'.

Kicking the cat

How often have you found yourself seething with anger from a bad day at work, after visiting friends or family or in the aftermath of essential household chores because of something someone has said or done to you? You get home, or into the car, and something snaps. Before you know it, you're screaming, throwing crockery at the walls or lashing out at your poor old puss, Socks. Maybe you did have a reason for striking out at your partner, for leaving dirty footprints on the kitchen floor, or the cat, for spreading feathers all over the living room. But the truth of the matter is that your explosion is more to do with what has happened before they came along and triggered it. You are taking out a load of accumulated anger on them, and indeed you may find yourself feeling relieved at discharging all that pent-up emotion. It's that relief that can make you feel justified in shouting. You feel better, so it must have been the right thing to do, which encourages you not to enquire further and to do it again next time. Or you may recognise what you've done and feel guilty, which is just as good a reason to try and seek justification and convince yourself that even if your partner or the cat was a scapegoat they deserved being shouted at anyway. You can then find yourself locked in a cycle of needing to convince yourself that it was their fault you had the argument and to go on having it. What's really going on is that you feel unable to shout at the people with whom you are truly angry – your kids, your boss, a relative, or some anonymous parking warden.

Transferring a legacy

Because we learn about relationships from our parents we often find ourselves copying them. When you, too, offer a hug and a kiss at the end of the day, or make your partner apple crumble, or run the bath when you know 'it's that time of the month', just as you saw your parents do for each other, this can be a joyous celebration of family continuity. But when you find yourself shouting 'You never listen to a word I say', and hear one of your own parents in your voice, it can be less helpful. What may be even more harmful is that you can find yourself replaying other people's arguments. If there were particular disagreements that came up in your own childhood, the mention of something similar may find you automatically reacting in the way you saw played out in front of you, with you and your partner now taking the role of the adults you used to watch. Arguments about who makes and spends the money in your relationship, or about sex, or about having a family, may well reflect what is going on between you. But equally, your pain, anger and a lot of the heat can have as much to do with loss and separation in your past than in the reality of the present.

Passing the buck

You can also find yourself fighting other people's battles. Alexia would fly into towering rages with her husband Peter whenever they had been to visit her parents, or her mother had been on the phone. Alexia's mother was highly critical and very demanding. She would criticise Alexia, and complain to her about Peter, whom she felt simply wasn't good enough for her daughter. After such visits or conversations, Alexia would find fault with everything and anything Peter did. She would shout at him for having left his dirty socks in the bathroom, for forgetting to order extra milk, for wasting money buying luxury toilet tissue instead of the standard type. As a final swipe, she'd also accuse him of being lazy, and lacking ambition or initiative. Alexia and Peter finally looked at their arguments, and did an exercise to explore the feelings behind their conflict.

What's this really about?

Arguments often seem to blow up out of nowhere. After a row, we often can't understand why we said or did what we did. This is an exercise to help you work out what triggers your rows. You need to explore what makes you angry, why it happens and when it happens. Arguments happen because a button gets pushed. Something is said or done and this sets us off, in anger, panic or grief. But the button isn't the reason in itself. You need to access what is behind this reaction by asking yourself, 'What's the button and what pushes it?'

You can do this with your partner or on your own. Sit down and remember your last argument. Don't replay the row – what you are looking to recreate are the feelings you had at the time. Close your eyes and get in touch with what made you angry and exactly how you felt. Be honest with yourself about this. It might be anger or rage – it might be fear, panic, grief, guilt. Then ask yourself the question, 'When have I felt like this before?' Go over your feelings both before and when you became angry, and after. Ask yourself what you were doing to deal with those feelings, and whether it worked.

Alexia realised that two things pushed her buttons. Her mother was someone who was very demanding. All through her childhood, Alexia felt she had to live up to expectations. She had achieved high marks in exams at school and a first in her university degree. She had gone on to a successful career. Her father was admiring but her mother could only give grudging praise. When she fell in love with Peter, her father took to him but her mother was horrified because he was a laid-back, relaxed man with a well-paid but low-status job. Whenever she spoke to her mother, Alexia found herself defending Peter's situation. But as soon as she was alone with him, she would lash out at him in exactly the same words as her mother used.

When she thought about it, Alexia realised it wasn't anger she felt but panic and rejection. She had tried for so long to get her mother to approve of her, and her mother's criticism of Peter felt, as it was probably intended to be, a criticism of her. It was as if her mother was saying that, yet again, Alexia had come second best. By passing on her mother's opinions, Alexia felt as if she was playing 'pass the parcel' with her mother's disapproval, getting rid of it from herself.

Alexia also realised her buttons were pushed by a second aspect. When she did become angry, Peter became quiet and distanced. The more she shouted, the quieter he became, and no matter how much she goaded him, he wouldn't respond. Again, when she looked at when she had felt this way before, she found it was in her childhood. She had never felt able to hit back at her mother's unreasonable demands and whenever she had been criticised she had become quiet and distant – and been told off for being sullen and sulky. Peter was reacting in the same way as she had done when she had been criticised, and this made Alexia feel very uncomfortable. Alexia came to realise that her anger was mainly misplaced, leftover anger from her own childhood. Once she realised what the buttons were, why they affected her and when they were pushed, she and Peter could deal with their own disagreements far better.

We talk with each other, even with the people we love, far less than we think. Cast your mind back over today, yesterday or last week and try to focus on what really happened between you and your partner on any one day. With your hand on your heart, how often can you say you sat down and had a real honest-to-goodness *conversation* with them? For most of us, it's a barrage of instructions, questions and statements as we rush around, dealing with day-to-day business. When we come home in the evening, many of us slump in front of the television, too tired to talk, or only able to talk about what we see on the screen rather than ourselves and our own lives. It adds up to very little and, most importantly, it's not what communication – a conversation – is really all about. In most interactions, the reality is that we talk *to* or *at* our partners and very seldom *with* our partners. What distinguishes genuine communication, whether you call it debate, conversation or just a good chunter, from any other form of interaction is that it is genuinely two-way. Communication is when you listen as much as talk, when you hear as much as be heard, when taking in the other person's point of view is just as important as putting your own ideas across. Communication is an exchange of ideas, not a transmission of instructions.

Breaking the chain

We can often get stuck in futile disagreements with our partners that never seem to come to an end or a resolution. No argument is as bad as the repetitive argument that goes nowhere, where you feel the other person isn't listening to you, or where one or both of you feel the other is simply nagging. If you find this is happening between you and your partner, that would be one very good reason to revisit and review the way you communicate with each other. It's more than likely that both of you could benefit from brushing up on your communication skills. However hostile the atmosphere may seem, or stuck you feel, there are ways of calling a halt to the process and of putting these old arguments to rest.

Having a constructive argument

There's nothing wrong with having a disagreement. The problems arise when it just leads to shouting, anger and further confusion. If someone is being accused of nagging, a common complaint in arguments, the chances are that their request is not being heard, either because the other person doesn't want to hear, or they aren't making themselves clear, or because the real demand is concealed. The trick is to make sure you are being heard and that you make yourself clear.

Sit down with your partner. Agree a set time for your discussion, so that you will spend the next thirty minutes, or whatever, talking it over together. Use a clock to make sure both of you get an equal share of speaking and being heard, and listening. Agree, too, to the following guidelines.

When you talk about what is bothering you, you have to say 'I'. It's supposed to be arrogant or selfish to use the 'I' word so we tend to be brought up to avoid it. When we want to make a point, in discussion or argument, we either claim 'Everyone' or 'All our friends' or 'Your father/mother' thinks so and so, rather than taking responsibility for those feelings ourselves. Or we put the responsibility on the other person, by saying 'You make me think or do such and such'. One important step to constructive arguing is owning, or taking responsibility for, our own feelings. So, using 'You', 'One', 'They', 'Everyone' – in fact anything except 'I' – is outlawed. There is a great difference in saying 'I'm angry because you don't tidy up the living-room when you said you would and that makes me feel you don't listen to me', instead of 'You're lazy, selfish and inconsiderate!' The main difference is that the other person may rightly object to being called names, especially when they might have had a reason for what happened. Once they disagree you will find yourself stuck in the circular argument. But no one can disagree with an honest explanation of your own feelings. And once they are explained, you may be well on your way to dealing with them.

Confront problems, not people. The argument should not be about the person, but what they do. When you feel upset, stop to work out exactly what is bothering you. Instead of shouting at the person, explain what your anger or upset is really about, then find a way of agreeing on a resolution.

Accept that you can't help what you feel, only what you do about it. Life and relationships aren't simple and most of us have a complex and mixed range of feelings about ourselves, our partners and our relationships. There are and will always be times when you feel upset, with feelings of anger, rejection, guilt, loss and need, even in happy relationships. Perhaps one of the most important messages we need to take on board is that negative feelings are as much a part of life as positive ones. They won't overwhelm or destroy you or your relationship, provided you deal with them. So accept your feelings, even if they are sometimes ones you would rather not own. Be honest about what you are feeling and why. You are not to blame for your emotions.

Accept that you are, however, in control of the actions you take because of your emotions. You are being dishonest if you say you can't help what you might do. Having gained some insight into why you and your partner may be having difficulties, you can pinpoint your own fears, angers or anxieties and come to understand them, and then work on strategies for making a change. Sometimes a 'pre-emptive strike' can nip problems in the bud before they really begin. Most relationships go through difficult periods, so don't despair. There are many things you can do to improve your life together.

Win–win

Your aim should be to turn every encounter into a win–win scenario. There are three possible scenarios in any face-to-face encounter.

Lose–lose. Both of you come away from the encounter feeling bruised, battered and that you have lost.

Win–lose. One of you comes away feeling triumphant that they have won; the other feels unhappy that they have lost.

Win–win. Both of you come away knowing both of you feel good and that the encounter was equally satisfying and successful for you both.

Win–lose scenarios may be the preferred prescription for a sporting engagement, when you might not feel anything was achieved unless one of you – preferably you – did better than the other person. But it's a losing formula when you apply it to personal relationships. Every time one of you walks away feeling diminished, the relationship itself has lost out.

Some people enjoy a good row – it gets the adrenalin up and the juices flowing – and some couples can fall into a pattern of using arguments to fuel their sex life. Others, thanks to their own backgrounds, feel that a row is a form of communication and closeness. And, of course, arguments can be addictive. If you and your partner find yourself reaching for the familiar shout, scream and slam every time you have a difference of opinion, it's worth looking at what you might be getting out of it. On one level, you might say or think that nobody has conflicts from choice. That is not necessarily true. There are distinct advantages to carrying on relationships through the medium of conflict. Do any of these ring true, and can they be forming barriers to you and your partner speaking to each other?

Pay-offs of fighting
Excitement
Every time you have a fight, the adrenalin surges and the spirits rise. An argumentative lifestyle is seldom boring and it can seem a lot more interesting than a calmer, more serene way of behaving. The adrenalin rush can quite literally be addictive and you can find yourself deliberately goading other people into a row or rising to the bait very easily, because you crave the physical sensation set off by getting angry or upset. In short, you can get off on anger.

Intimacy
An argument can feel a very intimate, close experience. When you are fighting with someone, you can be sharing feelings and secrets you might keep quiet about at other times.

Distance
Arguments, however, control the depth and extent of the intimacy you can have with other people. If you have reasons to fear getting close, you may trigger a row every time you feel you are getting near enough for you to feel vulnerable.

Strong feelings that seem like love
It's easy to trigger an argument but far harder work to build a loving relationship. Causing a row is a fast track to the expression of strong emotions, which bear a similarity to love.

Attention

When you're shouting at someone, or they're shouting at you, at least attention is being paid. If you don't trust yourself to be lovable or loving, having a row at least makes some sort of connection.

It proves they'll stand by you

If you fear that the people you love may leave and abandon you or cease loving you, an argument is a test. If they're still there afterwards, you may feel it's OK.

It proves you're right in feeling unworthy

If you fear that you're not good enough for the people you love, an argument gives you confirmation that you were right to feel inadequate.

You can see that any exchange goes so much better when everyone explains how they feel. When you can appreciate the other person's feelings and their point of view, several things happen. For a start, much of the anger and aggression of the encounter goes. Even when you don't get exactly what you want, you can at least feel you are being heard and understood. But when it becomes a dialogue, you may find that you – and at the same time, the other person – do make gains. Sometimes, the gains are only in being appreciated and heard. Both of you may feel better as a result. When a row is threatening, there are two last things for you to do. One is to pick your moment. The other is to take the IT TEST.

Picking the moment

It is important to pick and choose the situations over which you disagree. You'll 'win' more often if the fight is about something important. The more fights you have over trivia, the more often you will get tied up in destructive and futile arguments. If you keep the times you want to make a point or dig in your heels to the few occasions when you feel strongly, your partner is more likely to listen. Try this exercise to work out your priorities.

What are the things that really upset you with your partner? What are the things that just get on your nerves? And what are the things they do that you actually like?

Look at the emotions in your relationship as money in the bank. When you or your partner does something that pleases, it's as if you put a banknote in your account. When you have a row, it's as if you went into the red and into debt. When something annoys you, it's as if you took the money out of the bank and put it in your pocket, just waiting to blow it. If you're forever taking out, pretty soon the bank is empty and you have nothing left. Having disputes does less harm to couple harmony if you keep filling the bank as well as taking away.

Are you getting the balance right? Fill in the columns and talk over what you've written. Can you see ways to cut down on arguments and increase your emotional bank balance?

These are the things that make me angry	These are the things that annoy me	These are the things that make me happy

Take the IT TEST

If an argument is brewing, step back, bite your tongue and lower your voice. What often happens when we feel angry or challenged is that all our body language moves towards having a fight. We look away from the person, refusing eye contact, and this tells them that we don't want to talk this over. Or, we stare at them in such a way as to try to force them to back down. Our fists may ball up, our body becomes tense and we may stand up or step forward, taking their space. When we speak, our voice becomes loud and strident. We may stress what we say by jabbing a forefinger at them – a very attacking gesture. Next time the temperature rises, try the IT TEST – Invite, Talk, Time out, Explain, Stand your ground and Treat yourself;

Invite

Defuse what is happening by becoming aware of your feelings and the way you are showing them. Instead of folding your arms or pointing a finger, hold up both palms as if to say 'Peace! We don't want to fight.' Invite the other person to sit down with you and get on their wavelength, to sort this out together.

Talk

Talk it over. Don't issue ultimatums or final statements that prevent you working out a compromise. However unreasonable you think your partner is being, listen to what they have to say, and then ask them to hear you out too. Seek a solution that meets with both your approval, however difficult you may think that will be.

Time out

If the disagreement makes you hot under the collar or you need time to think, ask for a time out. But do not under any circumstances make this an excuse to try to brush the whole subject under the carpet. Agree a specific time when you can talk about this again, and use the delay to think it over and talk about it further.

Explain

Make a point of becoming very clear about what it is you want and what it might be that upsets you. There's no point in getting in a rage because you asked your partner to put petrol in the car Friday night and they haven't done so by Saturday lunch time, if you haven't explained that (a) you hit the panic button as soon as the warning light shows, or (b) you actually wanted it for a drive out on Saturday afternoon. If they're someone who doesn't feel it's necessary to fill up until the gauge is well down, and thought Sunday morning was time enough, the row is really down to a misunderstanding not their neglect. Define, explain and negotiate what are your requests and needs, and listen to their feelings on the matter too.

Stand your ground

Don't be deflected or put off. Your partner may ridicule, distrust or be hostile to your trying a new way of sorting out conflict. You may find that to begin with, using these methods of discussion and exploration may increase the tension and anger. You may also find it feels uncomfortable, if not positively unnatural. It takes hard work – waiting until they finish what they're saying just so you can butt in to say your pre-prepared speech is far easier than concentrating on listening to and hearing them. But the old ways don't work so it's worth trying these out, however hard – in practice and on your self-image – they may be.

'I did an assertiveness training course at work and I found so many of the lessons we had, about "I" messages and owning your feelings, and being clear, were such a help in my job. We'd been having a hiccup in our relationship so I tried them with my husband too. He dug his heels in. He seemed to go out of his way to be awkward, no matter how hard I tried, and said things like "Don't you think you can come home and use your smarty-pants techniques on me!" One day it all got too much and I just exploded. I said I wasn't trying to catch him out or use him as a guinea pig or anything, I just wanted to make our relationship better because I loved him. I said I thought we deserved as good as I gave to my job and since it worked there, I could be forgiven if thinking it could work for us too. He went very quiet. And the next time I tried it, he listened. Our relationship is so much better now.'

Treat yourself!

What stops you communicating with your partner are often leftover feelings of resentment, anger and lack of self-worth from your own childhood. If you want your partner to value you, and value themselves, the first step is to value yourself. Give yourself time off every now and then. After a hard day, take a break with a treat that's just for you. It may be an uninterrupted hour with the music or TV or radio programme of your choice. Or a soak in a hot bath, with a book and a drink. Or a glass of wine or beer with your feet up and the newspaper or a magazine.

Broken record

What happens when your partner simply won't listen or respond to any of these attempts at making contact? A useful technique for making a point and not being put off, when it's justified, is 'broken record'. Even when you do it 'right', you may not get the 'right' response. People, after all, are not robots and won't run the intended programme just because we seem to push the correct buttons. They have their own thoughts and agendas, and may need some time to see in what ways they too may benefit from our new style of sorting out conflict. If you're coming up against arguments for arguments' sake, or if they are just dragging their heels, don't allow yourself to be diverted or drawn into arguments, just be insistent. Keys to broken record are:

- Say something that shows you've heard. Recognise what your partner is saying to you and sympathise: I can see . . . you say . . . I realise . . . that may be how it feels to you . . .
- Be clear about what you want done.
- Don't lose your temper.
- Stand your ground.

'David, I asked you not to make remarks about me trying to diet in front of your friends. I want to lose weight but that's my business. I felt humiliated and upset when you made those remarks at the pub yesterday. Please don't do that again.'

'Oh, come on Julie, it was just a joke.'

'You may have thought it was a joke but I felt humiliated and upset. Please don't do that again.'

'Where's your sense of humour?'

'My sense of humour is fine, thanks. I felt hurt when you made those remarks and made me the centre of attention.'

'You're taking this too seriously.'

'You may think I'm taking it too seriously, but I felt very hurt. Please don't do that again.'

'Well, I'm sorry but I still think you're coming on far too hard about what was just a joke.'

'I can see how you might feel I'm getting at you, but please, I want you to realise how hurt I felt.'

'God, you're just doing this counsellor thing at me again and I hate it!'

'That may be how it feels to you, but I'd like you to hear what I'm saying and not do it again.'

'It really did get to you, didn't it?'

'Yes, it did.'

'Well, I'm sorry. That wasn't what I meant. I didn't realise how you felt. I won't do it again.'

Be polite, don't raise your voice or lose your temper. Persist, repeating the request and go on far longer than you might think would be comfortable. If you keep it calm and don't rise to any bait or argument, you will be surprised how many times you can simply repeat a message. If you're not getting anywhere, after as many attempts as you feel able to repeat, try one final time.

'I've asked you ten times and I'd like to ask you once more please not to make those sorts of remarks about my weight and my diet.'

If you then feel you are getting nowhere or are losing your cool, break off saying:

> 'OK, we'll leave this for ten minutes and then we'll discuss it again.'

Go away and congratulate yourself for not having lost your temper and for having left the door open for further talk. After ten minutes, go back. You may find your partner has thought about what you've said and has come round. If so, thank them without further comment. If not, resume and continue. If you do this without reproaches, complaint or threats and without getting hooked into arguing, it isn't nagging. It's making yourself clear. Your partner will get the message that you're serious, won't be deflected, drawn or incited to violence (verbal or otherwise) and will persist. Sooner or later, they are likely to hear you.

You can't eliminate arguments from your relationship. It's unrealistic to hope to, and possibly harmful. A relationship that doesn't have conflict is one that is dead. But if you follow these tips you can make rows less painful and the effects helpful rather than destructive. Prevention, however, is always better than cure. If you had a way of predicting when and why you might argue in the future, you may find ways of dealing with and heading off rows even before they begin. In the next section, we'll be looking at how you can do exactly that.

4

Crunch Points and Change

Relationships tend to hit problems at specific times in our lives, and in the life of a relationship. We call these times 'crunch points'. Crunch points are stages in your life when something changes, and change – whether it's planned or unexpected, welcome or troublesome – puts pressure on the balance of a relationship. Common crunch points for couples may be just after the honeymoon, during the transition to parenthood, when children start school, during their teenage years, when kids leave home, and at retirement. Individual crunch points that can affect a relationship may be at any of the significant birthdays (usually, those with a nought or a five at the end of them!) or at menopause or other signposts to mid-life (such as being told you need glasses, or noticing grey hairs). Crises may happen because of family obligations, marriages and weddings, and death in the family. Crunch points can be unexpected and their effect devastating. Couples whose relationships are jogging by fairly happily up to that point may be unable to cope when something comes along that breaks routine.

Most of us expect relationships to stand still, and think what we feel in the first flush of love will be how it will go on. The real problem with this, mistaken, belief is that when your relationship, your feelings for your partner and your shared sex life do change, you may think it's because something has gone wrong. You might assume you or your partner has fallen out of love, the relationship has soured or you've got a sex problem. In fact, all intimate relationships go through different stages and each has particular characteristics and pitfalls. Once you know what are the crunch points and are prepared for them, you may be able to cope with the various ups and downs in the life of any relationship. There is a wide range of distinct phases that you may experience, some because of changes that happen to every relationship and some because of changes that happen to every individual. If you look at each crunch point and explore the possible feelings and anxieties that may accompany it, you can then see how you may react, and how you could redress the situation.

Crunch point: First flush of love

The first flush of love is the period when you're walking on air, drunk with love and lust. You have butterflies in your stomach at the sound of your beloved's name, and your friends are probably sick to death of hearing it. You're convinced s/he is Ms/Mr Right and your dream lover. And you may be correct, at least about the 'dream' bit, mainly because the person you love is partly a fantasy. The 'high' of first being in love explains why some people become addicted to the intensity of that emotion. They fall in love with falling in love, and seem to be forever succumbing to someone new, in relationships that never progress beyond the first few weeks or even days. As soon as they begin to come down, they finish the relationship and go on to another, to chase the hit. If you're having sex, it's likely to be exciting and satisfying because you're so hyped up all the time that you're halfway there before you even touch.

As with most addictions, you develop a tolerance for the drug. If you think that this heightened state of awareness and emotion is how you should always be feeling, you're in for disappointment. Or, you're dooming yourself to having to chase an increased level of excitement with each new partner and each new love affair.

How to get through it

Enjoy it for what it is, recognising that the intensity is made up of excitement mixed with fear. First flush of love is a roller-coaster ride that has as much misery as enjoyment to it. It is perfectly normal to feel scared at leaving this stage to move on. When a relationship develops, you know the price for trust and love is being more vulnerable to the other person. You may want and need to reassure yourself that it is worth the risk, and that trying to continue at the first-flush intensity is ultimately rather boring. Do you really want to eat caviar and drink champagne at every meal?

Crunch point: The honeymoon is over

The problem with the first flush is that, by definition, it can't last. People who set this as the standard for what a relationship should always feel like end up being disappointed. Once reality bites, and you start the rest of your life, all those hyper feelings die away and reality can seem dull and boring in comparison. The temptation is either to chase that elusive 'falling in love' feeling by bailing out or by having an affair, or become bitter, angry or guilty, blaming yourself or your partner for what you see as a failure in your love life.

How to get through it

You can't retain the precise edge of the first thrill of falling in love – there's no point in pretending you can. But you can keep much of the excitement, with an extra special something that only comes with someone you really know. You can do this by consciously remembering the emotions and retaining the behaviour of lovers. Once the honeymoon is over, couples who retain a successful relationship often do so by taking the time and effort to court and please each other, however long their relationship has lasted.

Crunch point: Getting to know your partner

After the honeymoon is the time when couples start getting to know each other. You first fall in love with a construct – a mixture of the real person you've glimpsed, and the person you hope and imagine them to be. As you get to know them, you'll begin to see how they resemble and differ from the blueprint you carried in your mind, of the partner you wished for and need. It can be an exciting time, as you merge the image of the person you thought you loved with the real thing. But for some people it's difficult, frightening or disappointing, as they discover their partner isn't the person they thought. And for others, it's a time when they bury their heads, not wanting to accept the gap between reality and fantasy.

How to get through it
You can get through this period by being flexible and approaching it as a new adventure. That your partner may turn out to be different to the person you thought you fell in love with isn't the problem – seeing it as such could be.

Crunch point: Getting in deep

Relationships can founder just at the moment when partners seem to be getting really intimate. One member of the couple may be astonished to find the one they love suddenly pulls away, 'Just when things were going so well'. The other may be overcome with panic and doubt. Intimacy can make people feel totally vulnerable. When you open yourself up to another person, you increase the risk of being hurt, because the other person knows so much more that they can use against you. Most significantly, if you have experienced loss in the past, a deepening relationship will make you fear being abandoned again, as you might have felt you were once before.

Floella and Bebe had dated for two years before they moved in to live together. Six months later, their relationship hit problems.

'It was as if, one day he was telling me that he'd never felt for anyone what he felt for me. And the next, he told me he was confused and wanted a break from being with me,' said Floella. Floella was even more hurt and as astonished to discover that Bebe had started an affair three months before moving out. At the same time, he had been telling her he loved her and wanted to get married. When they saw a counsellor, it emerged that this was a familiar pattern for Bebe. He had had several long-term relationships, some of which just petered out. But the ones that had developed into something serious had ended 'out of the blue', soon after they had begun to feel important. Each time, he said, the relationship had been going well and he couldn't explain why he had the impulse to be unfaithful and leave. 'I found myself talking about my father and how much I loved and respected him,' says Bebe. 'I just hadn't made the connection but there was this memory I hadn't wanted to have but I couldn't get away from. On the day I broke up from primary school, my Dad spent an hour or so talking about all the things we were going to do that summer before I started secondary school, and all the things I'd be able to do when I was older. A week later, he and my Mum split up and he left us. I did see him, later in the summer, but we didn't do any of the things he'd promised. I don't remember doing it, but it's as if I swore nobody would let me down like that again.' Bebe drew away whenever he got close enough to someone to love them as much as he loved his father – and they gained the power to hurt him as much as his Dad had. When you feel that powerless and angry, it seems better to be alone but in control than in love and close to someone, and vulnerable. As soon as he knew he was in love, Bebe's unconscious defences took over to take him out of reach. The trigger for his fears was the very thing that most people find comforting and reassuring – the realisation of loving and being loved.

How to get through it

This is behaviour that can be confronted and challenged. Above all, if this is a pattern in one or both of your past relationships, don't let it become personal. In other words, if this relationship is heading the same way, the chances are that it is not because of anything either of you has done wrong or has failed to do; it's the past that is responsible. However, patterns can be changed, if both of you are prepared to talk about it and work at it. If fear of intimacy is a problem, it may need the help of a counsellor to explore the origin and reasons and work towards a solution.

Crunch point: Meeting someone new

It's easy to feel that the outside world no longer has any effect on you when you're loved and in love. Some people come to believe that having a relationship acts as a sort of vaccination and confers immunity to other people's charms. And that being one half of a partnership will similarly render you invisible or off limits to people other than your partner. You may also believe that there is and can only ever be one person destined to love and be loved by you. In fact, there are probably hundreds if not thousands of people with whom you could make as successful a relationship as your partner – and one day, you're going to meet one of them. Whether it's on the second day of your honeymoon or ten years into a relationship, meeting someone who could have been a partner can have you looking at your relationship and wondering if the grass could be greener elsewhere. If you think there is only one person for you, you may make the mistake of imagining you've got it wrong and should, immediately, leave your present partner for the new love interest.

How to get through it
The remedy is to recognise that you might have had dozens of people to choose from, all equally loving and lovable to you. But you've chosen one of them. Having invested time, emotion and effort in one relationship it's a bit futile to abandon it now, to start over again, just when you're reaping the real rewards of that partnership. And that's only looking at it from your own point of view. Perhaps the most persuasive argument for concentrating on

your present partner is that dabbling in another relationship for no other reason than that you were equally attracted to the new person would be underhand and hurtful to someone you love – your present partner.

Crunch point: Balancing work and home

Once the dust of the honeymoon has settled, you have to come to some agreement about how you are going to manage your day-to-day life. Most couples drift into an arrangement, without actually discussing it. You may then each take on responsibilities that are fair and suited to you. Or you may find you've accepted chores along traditional lines – he takes out the rubbish and cleans the car and she does everything else – and there's an unfair burden on one of you. In addition to that, living patterns change and your separate responsibilities in and out of the home may alter.

How to get through it
What functions and is fair at the start of a relationship may not be even-handed later. At some point you're going to have to face up to and allocate chores – or one (or both) of you is going to feel resentful and used. Talk it over!

Crunch point: Significant birthdays

There are certain birthdays that arrive with baggage in tow. Any with a nought or a five at the end of them can trigger feelings of anxiety, irritability and even anger. You may not realise it's the birthday that is doing this, which is where misunderstandings can arise as partners, friends and family want to celebrate, but the birthday boy/girl has mixed feelings. Quarter and half centuries and any other multiple of five may remind you that you're not getting any younger. There may also be other, more individual, landmarks that cause special distress.

Rebecca wanted to put an ad in the local paper and throw a large party for her husband Leon for his fortieth birthday. He became short-tempered and silent whenever it came up, so she gave in to his insistence that he wanted no special notice of the event. She was confused and hurt when, the day passing with just cards and presents, he then went into a sulk insisting she obviously didn't love him because she hadn't made the effort.

Discussing the row with a marriage guidance counsellor, Leon's ambivalent feelings about fortieth birthdays became clear. Theirs was a second marriage and his first wife had died of cancer, when both she and Leon had been thirty. During her final illness, she had watched her neighbour's preparations for a fortieth party, and wistfully said, 'Well, I'll never celebrate that, will I?' Leon's anger and guilt at being the survivor meant that he felt he shouldn't be allowed to celebrate his own fortieth however much he really wanted to do so.

When Leon and Rebecca were able to unpick the various meanings they had attached to this birthday, they could recognise Leon's clashing emotions about it. On the one hand, he wanted to be made a fuss of and for Rebecca to confirm her love for him by arranging a special occasion. On the other, he wanted to forget the whole thing because it reminded him of his first wife's death. It also made him feel old, particularly as his daughter was sixteen and his son twenty-one in the same year – both signposts that speak of maturity for the young person, approaching senility for their parents! Once they could recognise and discuss what had been going on in both their minds, Leon and Rebecca could take steps. They splashed out on a late celebration. But, more important, they filed Leon's reactions away in preparation for Rebecca's fortieth the following year. They now realise he would have mixed feelings when that arrives. They are, however, reassured in now knowing that his reactions are natural and normal and so can be dealt with.

How to get through it
Recognise that it is very common to have mixed feelings about traditional events that are 'supposed' to be celebrations. If you have misgivings, talk them over rather than pretend or try to sweep negative feelings under the carpet.

Crunch point: Managing money

Couples argue about money more than any other subject. In fact, when you wrangle about finances, you're often really arguing about other issues that you find it difficult to put a name to. A row about how much money each of you spends will probably be about how much you do or don't – or one of you feels the other does or doesn't – value each other. For that reason, when you have different ideas and priorities about how your joint income should be spent, you may be arguing about more than just cash.

> 'For a long time, I really resented the way Peta spent time and money on her cycling. It cost a bomb, money that I thought should be spent on the house, and she went out every Thursday night with her biking mates. While she was out enjoying herself I was building an extension. We finally had a really bad row and after she'd been to her for depression, our GP had us both in for a chat. We ended up talking lots of things through with her. She helped me see that the house, and having holidays together, were important to me so that's where I thought we should spend our money. But to Peta, her bike had always meant a lot. It's the only time she spends away from us, when she's not working I mean. She does deserve it and the money isn't that much, really. But I felt I was sacrificing "my" money for "our" house, and not seeing that in fact that was because I got personal pleasure in how our place looked. Just as much of a kick, in fact, as she gets from riding her bike.'

Couples may find it difficult if the woman in a heterosexual couple earns more than her partner. Inequality the other way has always been accepted as natural. Increasingly, however, there are couples where the woman either earns more or has a job with greater status than her partner. Whether it's status or money, unless this has been brought out into the open and discussed, the couple may find resentment on both sides can creep in. If she has been brought up to think, in her heart of hearts, that men look after women she can feel let down if her man doesn't take on that role. If he comes from a similar background, he may feel guilty and resentful at letting her down or at being superseded. In either case, the couple could find themselves arguing about plenty of other things when the actual problem has been swept under the carpet.

How to get through it

Whether you have joint or separate accounts, it can often be important for both members of a couple to have money they can call their own. You would both benefit from having even a small amount that you can spend on yourself without guilt. But it's equally vital for a couple to talk over their finances, to know what is coming in and what is being spent, and to agree a budget.

Crunch point: Planning for parenthood

Perhaps the most crucial crunch point of all is decision-making about pregnancy. In fact, parenthood is such an important, irrevocable step that most people bury their heads in the sand and totally fail to come to terms with it. To have or not to have – and if so, when and how many – is one of the great taboo subjects, something every couple should discuss and so many do not. The main problem is that we still operate from old ideas. We often don't talk about pregnancy prevention in the early days of a relationship, because it's seen as an embarrassing subject. Women don't want to raise it, because knowing about contraception implies a knowingness that 'good girls' shouldn't have. Men don't want to raise it because they're scared of showing ignorance or incompetence. We still live in a society where sex before marriage is said to be wrong – even though most of us do it. But while we do the sex, we shy away from admitting it out loud, by avoiding talking about birth control. This means that, by the time a relationship is well established, instead of using the increased intimacy between them to be able to raise the subject, many couples are in the habit of not talking about sex, birth control and pregnancy. We also assume that children arrive come what may and are something we don't really need to decide about.

> 'Of course, everyone has children – don't they?'
> We have the technology to make a choice but not the
> tradition of doing so.

We don't grow up expecting to talk this over with a partner, because it's not something we might have seen our parents' generation doing. Family planning may still not be totally foolproof, but it is pretty effective. When faced with choice, many people feel ill-prepared to make it, and often fudge the issue. Couples will feel anxious and not yet ready to move into being parents, but will take risks, in order to let fate lend a hand. Sadly, this also means that when couples do have very different feelings about the timing of a family or its size, lack of a model of how to talk about such decisions means that one or other will act on their own rather than talk it through.

How to get through it

You may never have the call to talk over what you'll do if you win the lottery, or a comet heads for earth, or you live to be a hundred. But every couple will have to face up to choices about childbearing. They will have to face up to whether they will or won't, or indeed can or can't have children – the sooner it's talked about the better.

Crunch point: Trying for a baby

Whether you've talked it over and made a conscious decision to try for a baby or just arrived at the decision, there is likely to come a time when pregnancy is a goal. With some people, this is a crunch point that passes without noticing because pregnancy occurs quickly. But for others, it's a crisis. Trying for a baby can transform something that was enjoyable in itself, an act that bound you together and allowed you to show your emotions for each other, into a burden. You can go off sex in a major way when you're trying to conceive. If you're longing for a baby and it's not happening, sex becomes a chore because you're doing it as a means to an end rather than enjoying it.

How to get through it

Even though every month and every ovulation seems like a precious chance to start that pregnancy, you need to take time out from baby-making to keep your relationship in good health. Set aside every other month as sex for love rather than sex for children. Forget all about the calendar and the temperature charts, and leap on one another only when, and every time, you feel like it. The kicker is that you may find this is the time you do fall pregnant!

Crunch point: Infertility

The non-arrival of a pregnancy has more far-reaching effects than simply meaning an empty cradle. Both men and women may believe their sexuality is in question. They may feel useless and inept, hopeless and helpless. This can have devastating effects on the relationship. A partnership can suffer sexually, as one or other can feel betrayed by their own or their partner's body, and either withdraw or become demanding. Lack of desire or an inability to feel pleasure in sex are common, as guilt or anger affects the sexual urge.

Relationships also suffer emotionally, as partners may feel let down or to blame and take it out on themselves or the other person. Frequently, when infertility is diagnosed, the main focus is on the physical situation – the inability to get pregnant and possible remedies for that. What is often ignored is how both the diagnosis and the treatment affect the individuals involved and their relationship. Often, a couple will get locked into pursuing a pregnancy as the only solution for their ills. The tragedy is that even if a baby is finally produced, the price may have been the intimate relationship of its parents.

How to get through it

If you do have any difficulties in conceiving, it's important to consider your emotional health as well as the physical side, and to seek help from a counsellor as well as a doctor.

Crunch point: Pregnancy

Being pregnant is like approaching a one-way door – you should know that once through, you can never return. Couples thinking about pregnancy often promise themselves and each other that they won't let having a baby affect their own, private relationship. This rather misses the point: a baby is a person, not an object or even a pet. You are importing a third person into your relationship and that cannot help but change the way you relate to each other, as well as a host of other things. The nine months of pregnancy (or the eight/seven/six months between knowing you are pregnant and the actual arrival of the child) can be a scary time. If you don't share your thoughts and feelings, each partner can find their fears, anxieties and expectations of parenthood and the child can overwhelm them. Some parents-to-be become jealous, fearing they will be second-best in their partner's eyes. Others throw themselves into the role of parent, looking forward, as they see it, to having someone who will love them and not leave them. The pattern of your own childhood can often unfold in front of you during a pregnancy. If your parents weren't 'there for you' when you needed them, or were even abusive, the feelings of anger, loss, pain and guilt may return, but this time associated with the child that is about to arrive. This is why some new parents find the role so frightening that they cannot face it, and leave at this vital moment. And why others are drawn to repeat the unhappy experiences they had, but with themselves in the powerful position of the adult.

How to get through it
Pregnancy is the turning point, the period in which you begin that shift from individual and couple to parents. To make the journey you need to recognise it is a transition from one state to another. You need to celebrate that journey, to accept that nothing will ever be the same, and that once you are parents you will have to make changes. The only choice you have, in effect, is whether you make the changes yourself or let them be worked upon you, beyond your

control. You, your partner and your relationship will be different, but 'different' need neither be better or worse – just different.

Crunch point: Mother and child

Maternity can have a devastating effect on your relationship and your love life. Even before the baby is born, couples may find a barrier being forced between them. Because she bears the baby, his involvement is often ignored by friends and family and by professionals. Men may now be encouraged to come to birth classes and be present at the birth, but their well-being, both physical and emotional, during and soon after pregnancy is usually ignored. All the focus and fuss is on mother and child, leaving husband/Dad in the cold. When the baby arrives, the tremendous upheaval of producing a new human being from her own body can result in a new mother being totally wrapped up in the child. In effect, she falls in love, and the last thing she may be interested in is her partner. He can feel left out, rejected and redundant as all her love and attention is focused on the baby.

How to get through it
New parents need to make a special effort to keep their love affair alive. Not only do you need to remember that this is a joint production, with a joint responsibility, but that you are still individuals in a twosome, and need and deserve time on your own and together.

Crunch point: Going back to work

Leaving your child to go back to work can be a wrench. In most relationships, one partner will have only a short break after a baby arrives, whether by birth or adoption, and can be surprised at how resentful they may feel at going out to work again while their partner gets to stay at home, involved in their child. The one staying at home, in turn, can feel resentful at being abandoned and that the other is resuming a social life as well as a work one. Both can think that the other is getting the better of the deal, and feel angry with this but also guilty at thinking so. If/when the primary carer also goes back to work, this can give rise to even further mixed feelings. Mothers particularly feel guilty at leaving their children to go back to work. The legacy of centuries of pressure to see child-care as a woman's job and home as a woman's place means that women are very prone to feel torn when they leave children in another's care, even when they are sure it is the best option for them and their family.

How to get through it
Be open and share your feelings (with 'I' messages as in '*I feel* really guilty/bad/upset . . . ', not '*You* don't know what it's like!'). When both partners know how the other feels, you can arrange a timetable that helps all of you adjust. If you're to fit in time being a couple, being a family as well as each having individual time with your child/ren, you will have to plan it like a military campaign. You're only going to manage that if you're pulling together.

Crunch point: Starting school

Children starting school can be the cue for much heart-searching. It is the end of an important stage in your life when your first child goes to school for the first time, and the end of an era when your youngest goes too. They are no longer your babies and are beginning the journey that will take them out of dependency on you to leaving home for good. Most parents will feel sad, scared and even angry. There may even be a temptation to have another baby, to put off the day. Parents often find themselves protesting that their children are far too young, too delicate, too sensitive to go to school. What they may mean is that they themselves are far from ready to let go. It feels like a loss, and can throw up memories from your own childhood of being cast out or rejected. Once children have started school, they make their own friends. In a surprisingly short time, these assume some importance and they no longer need you quite as much. Parents and parents' opinions may still figure large in their lives, but you may no longer be number one. Just as they learned to say 'No' to you at the age of two, children will soon learn to be themselves, with often disturbing effects on you. It's perfectly normal for kids to be nervous about making the huge step from home to dealing with other people, whether it's at nursery, primary school or secondary school. But the fact is that most children see this as something immensely exciting and something to look forward to, if they are allowed to do so. Children who shy away from joining in are often expressing their parents' fear. You're the one who is shy or scared but they act this out by hiding behind you. This is either because parents have had their own bad experiences and are now passing these on, or it is because parents may be going through a crisis at home and don't want their children to leave them. Kids, after all, can often function as a shield between their parents. Once they start school you may have to face your partner on your own without the excuse of having to look after the children all the time and you may have your own reasons for finding this difficult. When children are frightened of going to school, it could be because of what they are scared of finding there. Equally it could be because of what they are scared is going to happen when they leave you on your own.

Sandra remembers when she was seven:

'I hated going to school and would go through the whole list of headaches, tummy aches, sore throats, you name it, to stay at home. I told my Mum there was a boy who bullied me and there was, but that wasn't the real problem. The thing is that my aunt and uncle split up that year, and my parents used to fight. I think what was going on in my mind was that if I left my Mum alone for a day, I'd come back and it would all be different. Left on their own, with my back turned, they'd decide to separate and I'd come home to find him gone, just as my cousins found their Dad gone. It didn't make sense, I know, but I was terrified that if I went to school, something awful would happen. Things did get better at home and they put their marriage back together, but I never really got over my fear of going to school. When my youngest daughter came up for her first day, it overwhelmed me. I couldn't stop crying and that set her off. It took a lot of thinking and talking to understand where I was coming from and to put it right.'

Starting secondary school can trigger a repeat of all these fears for both parent and child, and cause arguments and depression in the family. Partners who had bad experiences in their own schooldays can find it particularly hard when their own children go to school. Sadly, you can often almost force a repeat of your own misery by expecting it to be the same for your children. Either you prejudice them, so they expect the worse, or you give them little skills in dealing with problems in a more constructive way. Whichever, their schooldays may well have you reliving your own, and have you rerunning the rows and unhappiness you might have had as a child, but this time with yourself and your partner.

How to get through it
Parents who were not helped to develop social skills when they were children can pass this lack on to their own kids. A child who doesn't feel confident can find the prospect of starting school or moving from being a big fish in a little pond at primary school to being a little fish in a big pond at secondary school absolutely terrifying. If you or your children have any anxieties about school, the first remedy is to look to your own emotions and relationship. You may need to bolster their confidence by working on your own. You may need to help them feel safe and happy in leaving you for the day by working on and strengthening your couple relationship.

Crunch point: Becoming a teenager

A son or daughter becoming a teenager is probably the biggest crunch point for all parents. One of the most important tasks for a young person is to form their own personality and learn to be themselves. They have to break away from their parents and develop the ability to choose friends, make decisions and be independent. This is not something that can happen overnight and it's not something they can leave until they move out of home. It is, however, something they have to do for themselves and in the safety of being with their parents. The way they do it is to see-saw wildly between being sheltered by you and doing their own thing. They'll swing between being childish, wanting to be looked after and cherished, to being adults (as they see it), being responsible for their own lives and choices. Kids at this stage will flaunt their bid for freedom, choosing to wear the most outlandish clothes and body decoration, be with friends who seem to challenge everything you hold dear and listening to music you hate. They will be striving to scare you, annoy you and disagree with you. And the more they get up your nose and drive you up the wall, the happier they'll feel.

How to get through it

The more secure you are in your own self-esteem, the more you can recognise that this is a normal part of growing up, the better you'll deal with it. One very important strategy is to think back to your own teenage years and to remember how you dealt with it and what your parents said. The chances are that you both went through exactly what's happening now, from the other side. Use your memories to make choices that would be best for both you and your teens.

Crunch point: Their first boy/girlfriends and their first sexual relationship

The cat is really likely to be among the pigeons when a son or a daughter has what amounts to their first serious romantic relationship and particularly when they move on to their first sexual relationship. You may find yourself reacting quite violently to the prospect and couples may have the further difficulty of disagreeing about their responses. Parents can find themselves getting quite distressed and angry to the point of being unable to discuss the situation rationally. You may come up with all sorts of apparently sensible arguments for why your son or daughter should not be in love with, and particularly not be having a sexual relationship with, this particular person or at this particular time.

It's worth considering very carefully how far your arguments are for your son or daughter's benefit and how much they may be for your own. Your son's or daughter's entrance into sexual maturity has plenty of messages for you. Your anxieties about their well-being may be because you are replaying the script about your own transition from child to adulthood. In wishing to protect them you may be wishing to go back and make it better for yourself. You can't rerun your own life but your fears could make it miserable for them. And your anxieties could also be based in envy and jealousy. Most important of all, their transition can be seen to force one of your own. We tend to feel that sex is only for the young and the beautiful. Your kids are old enough to have sex; that makes you too old. Noticing their sexual maturity can often push you into a sense of competition and rivalry and since we fear we may come off second best the impulse is often to insist that they be disqualified from taking part in the race.

How to get through it

At this particular crunch point you may find it helpful to sit down with your partner and perhaps some professional help to explore honestly and talk over your feelings about what is going on and what it means to you. When you've done that you may be able to approach a discussion with the young people concerned with clearer eyes. It's obviously preferable for young people to leave a sexual relationship until they are older. But your disagreements with them may not be the best way of achieving this. And they may not be quite as young as you feel they are.

Crunch point: Empty nest

When their offspring leave home a couple could find themselves embarking on a whole new lease of life. Sadly, the empty-nest syndrome often means the experience is of loss rather than renewal. Couples who have not made real efforts to maintain their own relationship while bringing up a family can be bereft. If you have put all your efforts and attention into your children and ignored each other and the couple relationship, once your children have gone you may feel that you are living with a stranger. If you've got used to carrying on your relationship through your children, once they've removed themselves there can be trouble. You may have forgotten how to talk about anything but the kids and their needs. You may feel nervous, unsure and uncertain about carrying on a one-to-one conversation or a one-to-one relationship. It can sometimes be a bit like starting all over again, and after twenty years you may have forgotten how. You may very well have both spent the last twenty years developing along very different lines. While the children have been with you, each of you may have acquired personal interests which you've never properly shared. Not only does this other person seem a stranger, but he or she may seem someone with whom you've nothing in common.

How to get through it

If you are reading this before the event, the message is not to let it go this far. Keep in touch and make the effort to have time for yourselves while the children are with you as a rehearsal for all the time together you will have when they are gone. But if you are reading this after they have flown, don't despair because it's never too late. It's perfectly possible to remake a relationship. After all, you've the foundation of knowing that you were once each other's best friend and have shared an enormous amount since. The trick is to accept that any fears and anxieties will be normal; this is a common situation and you just have to get to know each other again.

Crunch point: Getting on

Realising you're getting on can be a personal crunch point. Being told you need glasses or noticing grey hairs can have you recognising that middle age is creeping up on you. It's the time when your sex life can really seem on a downhill slide. Your body's spreading, so you don't feel as sexy as you once did. The kids are growing up, bringing home their own partners and making plans to leave home, which all makes you feel redundant and old. There is a lot of cultural pressure to see middle or advanced age as an undesirable state rather than a time in life that commands respect from others and relaxation from yourself. There are after all two points of view. One is that middle age can be a period during which you capitalise on all you've learned. You could see it as the time when your knowledge of and intimacy with your partner would allow you to do so much. The other view is that with more years behind you than in front, the best is over. Instead of looking forward, many people have a mid-life crisis that involves them in trying to go back. Both of you may be tempted to stray, to prove you can still attract other people.

How to get through it

Mid-life isn't the time to give up. We're all going to live to a hundred in the new millennium, so now is the time to kick-start your life again. Take up exercise to get your body back in shape. Try out a new interest to liven up your social, and maybe even your working, life. Use the fact that you know each other so well to try some bedroom tricks you might have been too embarrassed to experiment with when you were younger.

Crunch point: Losing a job/redundancy/retirement

One or both members of a couple leaving the job market can shake up your relationship considerably. Whether this is from losing a job or being made redundant or because of retirement, the effect can often be the same. If you are used to working for pay and no longer do so, you can feel as if a part of you has been cut out. You may feel a failure and become depressed and lost. You may find it hard to adjust to a different pattern and resent any suggestion of doing things differently because it would seem only to underline what is missing. If one partner is still out at work, he or she may start off sympathetic but become more resentful if the other is unsuccessful at getting more paid work or finds it difficult to adjust to taking on more home-based responsibilities. If both partners are at home, adjustments can be even harder. The one previously at home can feel that their territory has been invaded and that they have come under scrutiny. Instead of welcoming help they can be furious at the other for coming in and trying high-handedly to change things.

How to get through it

Recognise that this will be a massive change in your lives and plan for it, starting way ahead of the actual event if you can. Discuss your feelings about the situation and reframe it as an opportunity rather than a loss – less money, perhaps, but more time. Brainstorm the ways you share out responsibilities, and what you can do with the time you will be gaining.

Crunch point: Illness

Illness in a couple or in other members of the family can throw up all sorts of difficulties, most of them hard to acknowledge. Illness can be very frightening, even when in itself it is relatively trivial. When one partner, for instance, has lost someone they loved they might react with panic, guilt or anger to their partner or anyone else they love falling sick. The other partner may find it confusing and even highly annoying because they won't understand this out-of-proportion reaction – as indeed the one who is panicking may not either. It is not uncommon for a close and loving relationship to be split when one member falls ill. Instead of being supportive and loving the well partner may inexplicably retreat. The reason may be that they are absolutely terrified of losing the person they love as they might have lost someone in the past. People who are frightened of losing those they love often provoke the very thing they fear. The memory they are operating from is one of being powerless to prevent someone they love going. If they think it's going to happen again, the impulse may be to take control of the situation. In other words, to leave before they are left. Both partners may be surprised to have this suddenly happen because it can occur even when the illness itself is not life-threatening.

Illness can also provoke arguments if either or both parties have come to see it through their childhood as an effective way of getting love and attention. If, for instance, being ill was the only time that you were made a fuss of or cosseted, whenever you feel in need of care you may fall ill. This can often lead to a pattern of one partner suffering a string of minor illnesses, particularly when there is any stress within or outside the relationship.

How to get through it
Acknowledge and discuss the effect illness has on you and your partner, and on your partnership. Face up to fears and furies, and talk over how you may deal with it.

Crunch point: Death in the family

When someone close to you dies it can spark off a lot more than just grief. Death is still a taboo subject which means many of us are unfamiliar with it and have never had a chance to discuss the mixture of complex feelings that we may have. Losing someone close to you doesn't just make you sad; it can make you angry with them for having abandoned you and guilty for having such emotions. We commonly blame ourselves for the things we might have done or not done, said or not said to the person before they died. After a death we often go into a state of shock as the whole situation feels unreal and our emotions are in suspension. When this wears off we can spend some time in a state of depression, self-blame and anger before coming through it.

If you or your partner don't know about and don't anticipate these stages of grief it can cause a rift. One or both partners may feel rejected and upset by the fact that offers of comfort are shrugged off during the initial numb stage. They may feel confused and at odds when anger and blame set in. They can further be alienated by the fact that people recover from a death at entirely different rates and may still be in mourning several years after the event.

How to get through it

Loss can be most destructive if you have unfinished business with the person who dies. There is a common process that everyone goes through when they lose anyone close. Grief may be the obvious response, but it's also natural and normal to feel numb with disbelief at first and even to deny it has happened. Survivors often want someone to blame and feel guilty, angry and abandoned by the person who has died. It can take some time before they can overcome depression to reach acceptance. Going through the rituals of grief – attending a funeral or holding your own ceremony if that isn't possible – does help the process. If you haven't been able to tie up loose ends and say the things you wished you had, writing them down or saying them to a friend or another family member or a bereavement counsellor can also help.

Crunch point: Trauma in the family

Any change in the family circumstances can be traumatic and have members reassessing themselves. These don't have to be changes for the worse for them to be significant. Any event that makes some difference – a wedding, a house move or even a traditional family festival such as Christmas, Diwali, Al-Hijra or Rosh Hashanah or an anniversary of any sort – can have people tense and on edge. You can be taken unawares by the way your partner or yourself can revert most embarrassingly to feelings or behaviour more appropriate to your childhood when you're with your family. Old jealousies and old resentments can make themselves felt again and you may find yourself carrying on an argument that should have been put to rest years ago. This can affect a partner as a spectator, but you may also find yourself rerunning this argument with your partner who will have no idea why, all of a sudden, you are hurt, angry or resentful of them.

How to get through it

Ask yourself 'When have I felt like this before?' This will help you locate the real reason for your distress. Recognise that any significant event will have side-effects and accept this as natural and normal.

Crunch point: Unfinished business

There are frequent situations where a happy relationship can come under strain because of something from the past of both or either of the couple concerned. You may think that the past is dead and gone, but if an issue was not laid to rest this unfinished business may return to haunt you.

One common situation, for instance, is when there has been abuse. The present relationship may be happy and secure with no hint of coercion or cruelty, but the abuse survivor may find themselves reacting as if they are still threatened. Another common situation is where there have been long-term relationships which have ended, particularly where there are children from the previous partnership. Jealousy, fear of rejection and resentment can be present and result in disagreements and arguments, with nobody being able to recognise that the shadow of the past is what's causing them. The unfinished business may have been contained until something happens that suddenly recalls the past emotions or situations and causes this crunch point.

How to get through it
Finish the business. This may mean having and finishing an argument or discussion with someone from your past, or about something from long ago. Bringing it out into the open may allow you finally to lay it to rest. If the person you want to speak to is long gone, you can still get the matter off your chest, talking to an imagined image of them or by writing it down in a letter that you then burn.

Here is what happened to Sanjay:

'I had a lousy childhood. My father was a real brute who hit me and my brothers every single day. The day he died was one of the happiest days of my life, or so I told myself. When my Mum was diagnosed as having cancer and told she had about a year to live, I went to pieces. It was my wife's father, who has been like a father to me, who said I should tell her how angry I still was with her, and with my Dad. I told him he was crazy. She was a frail, sick old lady and no way was I going to upset her. He said I'd never rest unless I did, and so did my wife. I hadn't realised I was, still, angry with her until he said so, but it was true. I couldn't forgive her for standing by, but I didn't see it. It was just that I held her at arms length because of it. She was in hospital and I finally wrote her a letter. I was sure she'd just tear it up or pretend she hadn't had it. Instead, she hugged me and we had a long talk, about how bad she had felt and how much she'd always wanted to apologise. When she died, I felt awful but not as awful as I would have felt if we hadn't had that talk. As it was, I found myself thinking about my father and how much I wished he had not been the way he was. I went back to his grave and I told him I was angry and sad and disappointed. It felt silly but it also felt good. I grieved for them both when she died but I realised that I'd been grieving for him for years, really. Being able to have it out meant I could stop.'

Crunch point: Sexual problems

Difficulties associated with sex are surprisingly common. Sadly, they can arise both because of reactions to a crunch point in a couple's lives or create one. A change in sexual function can happen for a purely physical reason or because of emotional difficulties. It's not unusual, for instance, for men and women to find it hard to summon the desire to have sex however much they love their partner if they are tired, distracted or under stress. What is a perfectly normal and probably temporary reaction, however, can be seen as a sign of rejection or even infidelity by the other partner. It can be seen by the sufferer as proof of ageing, a loss of masculinity or femininity, and a source of self-blame or guilt. Couples frequently don't realise that certain illnesses and certain medical treatments can interrupt sexual desire. If it hasn't been discussed, as it frequently isn't, by their medical carers it can be one more burden that is difficult to deal with. However, loss of sexual function is frequently the outward show of internal feeling. Where any of the other crunch points might have caused a loss of self-confidence or created conflict, sexual problems may then provide one more stumbling block to communication and understanding.

How to get through it

If talking about sex has always been difficult, you may well need the support and guidance of a professional to break the ice, such as a Relate counsellor or psychosexual doctor or counsellor. But whether you do it on your own or with help, talking together is the only way to overcome these problems.

Crunch point: Infidelity

Having an affair is often seen as the most obvious barrier a couple could come up against, standing between them and a happy life together. Somehow every other crunch point is considered to be easily overcome, or more often easily ignored, while this one cannot be pushed to one side. In fact, infidelity is often the end result of trying to pretend that other crunch points don't exist. It's not something that happens out of the blue or simply because the opportunity presented itself. Even when an unfaithful partner claims their reason for straying was that sex was offered on a plate the real motives are far more complex.

How to get through it

Discovering or facing up to the fact that your partner has been unfaithful is probably the most painful experience possible in a relationship. However, it is a crisis that can be resolved. Some couples claim that an infidelity in their marriage allowed them an opportunity to forge a better and stronger relationship. Their argument would be that facing up to what happened and why made them appreciate each other better and gave them the chance to agree a better and happier partnership. Perhaps a better resolution is to pay attention to crunch points and their influence and deal with what they throw up before either of you go through the pain of an affair and its discovery.

The cycle of change

Change is inevitable in any life and any relationship. Change itself shouldn't be a problem. It often is, mainly because we're not prepared. We don't expect it and so we're not ready and able to cope with it. Knowing what are the danger points can help us deal with them, not least because we can understand that feeling under stress and unhappy at change is natural. We need low points in our lives, if only to allow us to enjoy the high points. If we expect and accept reversals, however, we can grow through them, and use times of stress to make us and our relationships stronger.

I'm worried about . . .
Looking through the crunch points that have been high-lighted, pick ten that seem relevant to you. These may be crunch points that have already affected you, or ones that ring a bell and so might affect you in the future. Think and discuss how and why these might be difficult and talk over ways in which you might deal with them.

Be SMART
Recognising, preparing for and accepting that change will come to your relationship is one way of dealing with the possible harmful effects of crunch points. Another is grasping the nettle yourself, and actually making changes when you realise that you've become smug about your partnership or are heading for problems.

But how can you make changes in your lives and relationships that work and that last? Most of us have had the experience of making resolutions that fail – usually because we expect too much, aren't clear about what we want or because the two of us are pulling in different directions. The way to do it is to be SMART. This stands for Specific, Measured, Agreed, Realistic and Time-related. When you and your partner want to look at your partnership, sit down together and use this five-fold plan to guide you.

Be Specific

It's no good saying, to yourself or your partner, that you wish *everything* was different, or that you'd like to be happy, or that things were 'The way they used to be'. Vague goals make for confused results – or no results at all. So look at what you feel is wrong and come up with a specific issue you'd like to be different.

Measure it

Choose to change something that you can actually test out as having altered. You can't usually measure whether you feel happier or more of a couple, after a week or two. But you can see whether you've thanked each other every day, or done a particular task.

Agree what you're to do

It is true that the action of just one of you can affect the whole balance of a relationship. So, if one of you makes a determined effort to be more loving, more communicative, more assertive, the other has to adjust to a certain extent. But the truth is that for a relationship to change, both parties need to be pulling the same way. If you want to make changes, talk it over and agree what you'd like to be different and how you're going to get there.

Be Realistic

You can't hope to change the world and your relationship overnight. If you've got out of the habit of talking, don't make the resolution that you'll throw out the television and hold marathon chatfests every night. You're likely to fail and give up in despair. Choose a small goal that you can see as within your reach – such as switching off for a half hour to tell each other what happened to you that day, and discuss what you're going to do tomorrow. Do it, and if you find you go over your set limit, that's fine. Extend your boundary gradually. If you make small, realistic gains, you'll find you get the big goals eventually, and often faster than you thought possible.

Time-related

Change isn't going to happen if you say 'We're going to do this . . . sometime'. Just as you need to be specific about the What, you need to be exact about the When. So choose your action, and put it in a time frame: 'We're going to do this, at such-and-such a time, or by such-and-such a time.'

Hashmad felt her relationship with Ahmed had been going downhill for a long time. They'd bicker about what was wrong and both would end up feeling angry and got at. When she and Ahmed got SMART, they brainstormed what both of them felt they would like to change. Hashmad said she no longer felt loved and noticed. Ahmed felt ignored and rejected. When asked to come up with one request that might make a difference, Hashmad asked if he would bring her breakfast in bed on a Sunday morning. Ahmed used to do this and she said she missed it. He said he'd like to, but in return would ask that Hashmad acknowledge it. He'd stopped because she either said nothing, or complained about what he had brought her, saying she was on a diet. So they agreed he'd bring her a low-fat breakfast on Sundays, from the following weekend. Hashmad was touched and delighted – and said so – when he arrived with a tray, complete with red rose.

After a month, Ahmed had delivered breakfast every weekend morning and Hashmad had thanked him every time. They then went on to talk about other parts of their life together that had changed for the worse, such as the fact that they hadn't made love for five months. This was, in fact, the real point of the argument. Hashmad said she avoided sex because she felt overweight and unattractive, and Ahmed was able to say he loved her whatever she looked like – and he felt she looked pretty good, anyway. They brainstormed a SMART solution. They agreed to go to bed early that evening and to start with a kiss-and-a-cuddle, rather than planning full-scale orgiastic passion. Next day they were able to talk about the fact that they had done what they had agreed and had both welcomed getting back in touch with each other.

If you don't accept and allow for change, you and your partner can wind up having problems. But however painful and difficult, even the stormiest disagreement can be resolved, if you approach it with the right understanding and attitude. In the next chapter, we'll look at how you can solve relationship problems, whatever their cause.

5

Solving Problems

We don't stay the same, from birth to death. We grow from a collection of cells to a baby, through being a toddler, child, adolescent to adult. Tiny hands with perfect, miniature nails grow chubby, then smooth and mature, to aged, wrinkled and liver-spotted. Our personalities develop from being the delightful if exasperating self-centred naivety of the child to the infuriating self-centred naivety of the adolescent and – we hope – the more balanced adult. Everything changes – your body, your friendships, yourself.

> The one, single mistake that can doom you and your loving relationships is to expect or insist that anything will stay the same. Life is about change and transition.

You grow, and as you do so you develop your tastes, your

preferences, the way you look at the world and those about you. A successful partnership is one that celebrates and makes allowances for this, one in which each partner permits themselves and the person they love to alter. Your relationship will last if you make room for change. If you try to stop yourself or your partner altering, or ignore the changes that do occur, you will not thrive. Neither will yours become or remain a healthy relationship if you grow apart, losing touch with each other. Relationships often come apart, messily and miserably, because a couple refuse to let in change. Or, when change creeps up on them, they refuse to acknowledge and deal with differences.

Ten ways you can tell your relationship is going down the pan

Tolstoy, in Anna Karenina, said 'All happy families resemble one another; every unhappy family is unhappy in its own way.' He got it only half right. In fact, while each person and each relationship may be unique, when relationships are in trouble they often follow a similar pattern of breakdown. Relationships unravel slowly and inexorably, following an almost predictable process. In fact, there are ten ways you can tell your relationship is heading for trouble.

1 You begin to see cracks in your partnership. All those funny little habits that used to charm you – the way he sucks his teeth when he's annoyed, the way she always forgets to put the top on the toothpaste tube – begin to drive you up the wall. But you bite your lip and try to ignore your feelings.

2 The cracks in your relationship start to widen. You may begin to feel depressed or irritated or suffer frequent, minor illnesses. You may drop a few gentle hints, or niggle at your partner, but not enough to really cause rows.

3 Your relationship starts to disappoint you or to make you feel unhappy and dissatisfied. You look for and find something outside to occupy your time, fulfil or distract you. It could be an interest such as a sport or a new job or further education. It could be becoming involved in family or voluntary work. It might

be something more harmful such as abusing drink or drugs.

4   You pull yourself up short and try to involve your partner in your new interest, to share your life and interests with them again.

5   Involving your partner in your new interests or the fact that you have been pulling away from them having failed, you begin to make your misery more open, with arguments and complaints, both public and private, and more time spent on your own interests.

6   You find someone outside your partnership to talk to, to listen to your unhappiness and be sympathetic. It could be a friend, a family member, a professional such as a counsellor, GP, lawyer or member of a religious faith – or someone with whom you develop a new romantic and/or sexual relationship.

7   Your relationship/s with people other than your partner become closer and more intimate than your relationship with your partner. This may involve a romantic or sexual affair.

8   You realise your relationship is effectively over, as far as your feelings for your partner are concerned, although you may still be living with them. You mourn the loss.

9   You come to terms with the ending of your relationship.

10   You end the relationship and leave.

The process of unravelling

There are two important and significant aspects to this process of unravelling. One is that one partner can get right the way through to Stage 10 before the other may recognise or acknowledge what is happening. If one of you simply doesn't want to see that there are problems that need to be addressed, if you can't, won't and don't admit that your relationship is in trouble, it is possible to claim total surprise and lack of awareness up to that point. It does take a lot of hard work, mind you. You'd need to close your eyes and ears to fairly heavyweight evidence of unhappiness, both on your partner's part and probably on your own. Plenty of people do it, though, mainly because they'd like to believe that if they ignore all the signs of trouble, it will go away. The bottom line is that it would be far less work and far less pain to face up to problems and deal with them before you reach the point of no return. Counselling organisations such as Relate report that some 50 per cent of the couples who ask for counselling do break up. This is not because counselling doesn't work, or that relationships that hit problems are doomed. It's because couples with relationships in trouble almost always leave it too late to ask for help. You could rescue a relationship right up to Stage 8. In fact, you might even pull one back from Stage 9. But the further along you are, the more one of you has adjusted to the idea of living without the other, the harder it is.

The other significant aspect is that people can go through these stages at different rates – one of you may be at 3, the other at 5, at any one time. And you can stick at stages, reaching Stage 4 or 8 and staying there for a considerable time. You may also drop back one or two stages and then advance again. Couples can both be at the last-but-one stage after ten years of marriage, for instance, and go on to see their twenty-fifth wedding anniversary together. Emotionally, they may be living in a shell relationship, one which has very little closeness or sharing. As far as everyone outside is concerned, it can be the perfect marriage.

There is hope for you yet

If you can recognise yourself in these descriptions, the good news is that there is still hope for you to intervene and remake your relationship, if you are prepared to make changes. This isn't as easy, it has to be admitted. When I trained as a Relate counsellor, I found much of what I was learning in theory to help other people had lessons for me and my own relationships too. I started putting it into practice – and came up against a sharp slap in the face with a wet fish from my family, who with one voice said, 'Don't you come the counsellor with me! What do you think you're doing, bringing your Relate techniques home?' If you want to make changes and are looking to this book for support and suggestions, you may find similar difficulties. It's not always easy to face up to or understand your own behaviour or feelings, or alter the way you talk and relate to others. It can be uncomfortable and embarrassing to change, even when you are convinced it's the right thing to do. Other people, who haven't taken that first step of recognising there are problems or the second one of deciding to do something about them, will find it that much harder. It may be hard work, it may initially seem to cause more problems than it solves, but the fact of the matter is that using communication skills to improve your relationship really does work. It's also never too late to start because in a lot of ways it's retroactive. When you go through the process of looking at your own background and feelings and how that has affected you in the here and now, you can go back and rectify a lot of the misunderstandings of the past. It only needs the first step, which is for you to take responsibility for your own feelings and for action.

First, we need to explore our own pasts and understand ourselves. Take the time to heal your own childhood disappointments and boost your own self-esteem and confidence in order to 'break the chain'. Once you have an insight into what underlies your relationship you'll be able to see what you expected and needed from your partner. You may then be able to identify key behaviour patterns that pass on important messages, and can choose to strengthen or to modify them.

Problem-solving

A relationship without open conflict is not necessarily a relationship without problems. Every living and developing relationship will have points of difference. If you don't disagree it means that conflict is going on under the surface, where it can be truly destructive. The best thing you can do in a relationship is bring your arguments out into the open, where they can be dealt with and resolved. When you hit a point of disagreement or conflict, the first thing you need is calm. Call a time out and agree you'll work through a three-point plan.

When you hit a problem in your relationship, most of us

do one of three things. Either we run around like headless chickens, convinced the world has come to an end and nothing will make it better. Or, we take up the Ostrich position and stick our head in the sand and hope that if we ignore it, it'll go away. Or we get angry and blame someone else. Some of us manage to do all three, simultaneously or one after the other. In fact, the first three things you should do when you realise you have a problem, are these:

1 Ask yourself
What has changed?
We usually think or say problems come out of the blue, completely unexpectedly. This isn't true. What often happens is that there is a shift in our lives that throws us off balance – we just don't realise it at the time. It might have been something in your own life, such as reaching a significant age, losing a relative or starting a new job. Or it might have been something in your partner's life, such as missing an opportunity at work. Or it could be someone in the family, such as a child starting school. Before you know it, you're feeling angry, depressed or upset and arguing about anything apart from your real anxiety. Tracing back to when the troubles started could give you some insight into what you're really arguing about and so how you might be able to settle it.

When have I felt like this before?
Because arguments are often replays from our earlier lives, it can help to locate the feelings we're experiencing. Are you feeling panic, anger, rejection, hurt, fear? Is that how you felt years ago when something happened in your family to make you feel miserable or scared? Feelings at the moment are often tangled up and increased by echoes from the past. What happens is that an event recalls a previous episode, particularly if you've never been able to put your upset about that to rest. Anger, confusion or grief may still be floating around from that earlier life. When a similar event happens, you get hit with a double dose of bad feeling – the emotions from the present, plus those from the past. Realising what

is happening and disentangling the two streams of feelings can help you get a handle on your unhappiness.

What would I like to be different?
Imagine yourself in a better place. Picture what it would be like not to have this problem, and then tease out what exactly would be different. When you do that, pick out each, separate part of your life that would be different and then focus on what you need to do to achieve that.

2 Talk to your partner
Talk over with your partner what they might think has changed, whether they have had similar feelings before and what they might like to be different. Couples often stop themselves improving their communication by being convinced the other wouldn't listen or co-operate. What stops us is fear of being made vulnerable, of being the one to show our emotions and need. We also avoid trying to change because until we have tried, there is always hope. The anxiety is that if we try and it doesn't work, we really are stuck. But our partner is probably sitting there with the same fears, and the same wish to make it better. We don't know they won't agree if we haven't tried – and it is always worth asking.

3 Ask for help
If you broke your arm, you'd go to a doctor. If your car broke down, you'd probably call in a mechanic. Yet when we experience relationship problems, many of us shy away from asking for help. There are certain misgivings and misunderstanding we have about counselling and counsellors that can put us off. One is that counselling is interference in the private affairs of a couple, another that counsellors tell you what to do. Neither is true. Counsellors aren't nosy people who want to pry into your affairs. Their job is to give you the space and attention to allow you to talk. When you spill out your concerns, you often find you can see a solution. The counsellor helps you make sense of what is happening, to explore, understand and ultimately change it.

Counsellors never tell you what to do. They guide you in telling yourself, and the process is always in your control, at your pace and to suit you. It isn't 'washing your dirty linen in public' because the only person involved apart from you is the counsellor, who promises complete confidentiality. In fact, most of the excuses people put up against going to a counsellor boil down to one genuine statement, which is 'The thought of it scares me witless!' We're mostly scared of letting all those frightened, angry, damaging emotions out of the bag. We're terrified that these emotions will be overwhelming and that once we start crying or shouting we'll never stop. But the main skill and help that a counsellor offers is safety. A counsellor keeps all those feelings contained and in check, allowing you to get them out in the open and to deal with them. Far from letting them loose to wreak havoc, going to counselling allows you to release ugly or sad emotions and so let them go.

What's your problem?

Focus on yourself and your partner, either together or with the help of a counsellor, in order to work out what's your problem. This may not be as obvious as you think.

Will and Sandi had frequent arguments about money, who did the washing-up, and Sandi's leaving dirty coffee mugs in the living room. They never seemed to be able to settle their arguments and began to realise that the reason was that they were not actually addressing the real problem. They needed to ask themselves what they were really feeling when they quarrelled and what they were actually arguing about. One way of identifying problems, is to have a Think Tank discussion.

Think Tank
A Think Tank is a face-to-face discussion where you speak and listen with respect and honesty. There are three main rules to make a Think Tank discussion work.

---

1 Owning what you say

The most important rule is that you have to 'own' what you say. That means, everything you put forward has to be your own thoughts and feelings and you should acknowledge them as such, using 'I think' or 'I feel'. Don't evade by saying 'So-and-so says' or 'Everyone knows' or talk about what other people do or what you think they think. You can talk about how your partner's behaviour affects you, by saying 'When you do such-and-such, I feel . . .', but the aim is to put your point of view, not to criticise or attack them. Remember, the key is confronting problems, not people.

2 Turn and turn about

Take an equal turn to speak and to be heard. Listen without interrupting and use reflective and active listening to make it clear you are taking in what your partner is saying.

3 Agreement

The eventual aim of your discussion is to find a space where you both feel that you have been heard and appreciated. There should be no winner or loser, but an all-round agreement on the outcome. To that end, neither should shout the other down for what they say. Discuss the points rather than arguing with the person. Set aside time for this discussion so that both of you have a chance to have your full say.

When Will and Sandi did a Think Tank, it became clear that it was neither money, washing-up or dirty cups that was actually the point of their rows. Sandi felt that Will never listened to her or respected her opinions and Will felt he was expected to be the Man of the House, looking after the money and making all the decisions. Sandi responded by being an untidy child again.

Who's the baby?

We looked earlier at the way we often find ourselves falling into roles within a family. You can be the Good Child, Mother's Little Helper or the Bad Sheep. Your role often depends less on your own behaviour than on family scripts and the beliefs or needs of other people in the family. You may also find yourself reacting to your partner in certain ways because of another form of role expectation. We tend to relate to people in one of three ways: we can be Adult, Child or Parent. Adults take responsibility and face up to reality. Children dodge responsibility and rely on everyone else. Parents look after other people. Each role not only guides the behaviour of the person acting in that way, it also affects the people around. So, if you act as a child, your partner may find themselves becoming parental. You're stamping your foot and refusing to do your chores while they tell you off and clear up after you. The more you act the child, the more they may act the nagging, superior parent. But the more parental they become, the more childish you may be. It is, in effect, a closed loop. If you 'look after' your partner and deny them the chance to take responsibility, they have no incentive to be other than a baby. In contrast, if you act as an adult to another person, they too may be drawn to be adult rather than child or parent, too.

When Will and Sandi looked at what was happening in their relationship, they realised the problems were actually about mutual respect and expectations about the roles men and women have in a modern relationship. Will thought that to be a 'good' husband he had to look after Sandi and not let her worry about the sordid facts of life such as bills and budgets. The more he cosseted and cared for her, the more she kicked against his stifling behaviour that reminded her of a Victorian father. He acted the Dad so she acted the petulant kid.

Of course, there are times when it is healthy and appropriate for us to be parental and even childish. Running around naked in the moonlight is childish but fun, and asking your partner to clean up their mess when it's time to make the evening meal is parental but necessary. It's really just a case of what suits the time best and not getting stuck into always being one or other, all the time.

Brainstorm a solution

When you feel you have some idea of what is behind your problems, the next stage is to find a solution. One way to do that is brainstorming. Brainstorming is a game or technique that really helps you identify problems and come up with solutions. It can also break the ice and have you laughing as well as talking together.

In a brainstorming session, you both get an equal chance to speak, and every single idea you come up with is given equal weight – nothing is out of bounds. *Any* solutions can be put forward. Get a pad of paper and a pencil and set yourself a time – twenty minutes is usually enough to get the creative juices going but not so much that you run out of steam. At this stage, what is most important is that the solutions need not be sensible, workable or even desirable. Jump in with as many ideas as you can, and write every single one of them down *without comment*. 'Cut up Sandi's credit card', 'Stop worrying about money – it's there to be spent', 'Throw away our coffee mugs and plates and use disposable ones instead', 'Set aside some mad money every week', 'Have a rota for chores and have penalties for flunking', 'Agree a budget'. Don't sneer, laugh at or try to discuss any of these ideas at this moment. You'll find out why silly suggestions are welcome in brainstorming when you go on to the next stage. Once the time limit is up and you've put all your ideas down, take a break. Then, start at the top of your list and talk each one over. Don't dismiss anything out of hand, but do discuss what you think about it. Why not, in this instance, accept the 'Stop worrying' solution? What would be wrong with disposable crockery? The key to brainstorming is that, hidden among all the jokes, dross and rubbish, you are likely to find a gem you might otherwise not have discovered. Done properly, it also allows both of you the chance to feel brought together in the search for a solution. It can, above all, allow you to act adult-to-adult together.

Brainstorming works because:

- you do it together
- it's fun
- it helps you think of difficulties as challenges that can be overcome, not problems that can't be solved.

Drawing up a contract

Having brainstormed and discussed, you need a clear way of keeping track of what you agreed needed changing and how you've agreed to go about it. To do that, you should draw up a contract. This may seem over-formal and feel a bit silly. But having to look at what you've agreed in black and white and keeping it to refer to does help you stay up to scratch.

Making an agreement

The idea is to write down exactly what both of you have said they will do. The key is that it shouldn't be one-sided, with one person asked to make an effort or making changes and the other acting as usual. Work out a fair exchange and one you can agree. Make a precise record, including:

- what you've both agreed to do
- how you agree to do it
- when you agree to do it by
- for how long you have agreed to do this.

Both of you should sign the contract, and each has a copy. Review the contract and the agreed changes regularly. If the terms are not being met, discuss why and whether the contract needs to be redrawn or whether something needs to be adjusted.

Talk it over

What if you're having difficulties even starting to talk about your problems, let alone seeking solutions? Conversations often seem dead in the water before we even begin them. How many times have you approached your partner, burning to talk about something, only to have the door slammed in your face at once? One reason for this could be your manner. There are two ways of drawing out another person. The first is what is called the closed question. It's a conversational gambit that actually stops conversation. This is when you ask a question that can, and sometimes can *only*, be answered with a yes, a no or a very short statement. 'Was work OK today?', 'Have you called your mother?' or 'Are you watching the football tonight?' are good examples. Even worse is the question that assumes the answer you clearly don't want, such as 'And I suppose you'll be expecting me to drive tonight?' or 'So who has to walk the dog this evening?'

Here are some examples of closed questions:

'All right, then?'
'Was the bus on time this morning?'
'What do you do for a living?'
'Are you going away for your holidays?'
'Lousy weather, isn't it?'

Some closed questions go even further, by setting up the atmosphere for a fight. A phrase such as 'And what sort of time do you call this?' can't be answered, except in a way that leads straight into conflict. We use them as a smokescreen. They're intended to be a challenge and an attack, but by making it a question we can always then claim that the first blow was actually struck by the other person.

An open question carries with it a different message. Some examples of openers would be:

'Tell me about your day.'

'You look as if you enjoyed your night out. What was the best thing about it?'

'You look a bit down. Tell me about it.'

Turn these closed questions into openers:

> **EXAMPLE**
> *Closed:* 'You're not going out to the pub again, are you?'
> *Open:* 'I was looking forward to spending some time with you. Could we set aside some time to be together?'

Closed: 'What the hell do you think you're playing at, repairing your motor bike on the kitchen floor?'
Open:

Closed: 'Why can't you ever put your shirts in the washing machine?'
Open:

Closed: 'Why must you always look such a mess?'
Open:

Communication between you and your partner may be difficult for a number of reasons. It's not because you don't want to understand each other but often because you find it hard to begin. By the time you realise there are problems, barriers may already have gone up between you. When we are unhappy about being in touch with our partners, we stop communication in a variety of ways. One is through body language.

Body language

Often the main cause of a row is not what we say but how, when and why we say it. We pass on as many messages through body language as we do through words. Research shows that the vast majority of the information passed on in a face-to-face conversation is non-verbal. Only 7 per cent of the impact of any contact between two people is through what they actually say. Your tone of voice conveys 37 per cent of the message. But a massive 56 per cent is dependent on body language. If we want to communicate we need to check out what we are saying, what we want to say and what we'd rather we weren't saying in our actions as well as in our words. Your voice, the way you are standing, the little gestures you make all have more to say than what you actually said in words. When you go on cooking the evening meal/fixing the car/watching TV when your partner wants to talk to you, you say several things. You tell them you aren't interested in them. You tell them they are less important than the job in hand. You tell them their concerns are trivial. You tell them they aren't worth bothering about. You tell them your relationship can take a back seat. When you sit with your arms and legs crossed, you tell your partner that you are putting a barrier between the two of you. In effect, you guard yourself against them and their words. Sometimes, this is because you are frightened and feel threatened by them. Sometimes it is because you simply don't want to listen to them. If you want to be open to their words, you need to show them this by sitting or standing in a way that passes a listening message. This means making eye contact, not folding your arms across your body, and sitting with yourself pointed towards rather than away from them.

With body language, go tone and the way we use emphasis and language. You can entirely change what you say and what you mean by altering the 'voice' of how you say it. A simple question ('Are we going out tonight?') or statement ('I like your new jeans') can convey anything from the straight truth of the written meaning, to disgust, anger or criticism. Mixed messages, when the words say one thing and the tone says another, can be deeply wounding. The real problem with using sarcasm and other ways of altering a message is that it's dishonest. We use it because we can put a nasty, angry and critical twist to our words, reserving the right to deny what the other person understands by our remark. 'Oh, don't you look a picture!' 'Don't you like the way I look?' 'Did I say that?' Sarcasm is one tiny step away from bullying. It's only an acceptable form of interplay if:

- there is no intent to wound or put down;
- both of you use it equally and both see the joke;
- there are no hidden messages. If you can't say it openly, you shouldn't be saying it this way.

Touchy-feely

Physical closeness between a couple – touching, hugging, kissing – says more than just 'I love you'. It also passes on messages of how acceptable, or not, we think we and they are. In some relationships, partners do find it hard to be demonstrative, especially in this country with its tradition of 'stiff upper lip' standoffishness. 'Loves yer, course I loves yer, I'm here with you, ain't I?' is the watchword. It's assumed that partners know they're loved, without your needing to go all soppy and touchy-feely to show it. Not so! We need to hear it, to feel it and to show it at all times.

> Love is . . . always having to say you're sorry.

When your partner doesn't show his or her feelings openly, you feel unloved. More important, you feel unlovable and can often assume that the reason for the lack is your own bad behaviour or in-built badness. What anyone and everyone needs is unconditional love – to know that the most important person in your life loves you, no matter what. And you can't know that if they don't show it. If you missed out on being loved and approved of in this way as a child, you may find it hard to believe in; both hard to give and hard to receive. But it's never too late to learn the benefits of loving openly. Unlike a pot of money, an emotional gift does not impoverish the giver. In fact, you've got it, you give it, and you've still got it! Loving unconditionally is not the same as being a doormat. It doesn't mean always accepting what your partner does, but who and what they are. It means operating from the standpoint that both you and your partner are acceptable, good people who deserve to love and be loved. It means recognising that we can all behave foolishly, selfishly, badly at times but that does not mean we are foolish, selfish or bad.

Infidelity

Relationships come under strain when partners become distant from, angry with or hurt at each other. However, the single most painful and damaging discovery for one person to make is to find out their partner has been unfaithful. Affairs are surprisingly common. An estimated one in ten women is having an affair at any one time. Overall some forty in one hundred wives admit to at least one affair in their marriage. Half of those say they have had two or more lovers. In contrast, fewer men have affairs – around twenty-five in one hundred are unfaithful. But when men do stray, they do so more often, having from five to more than twenty lovers.

Why do people have affairs? Some say that it's because human beings – and particularly men – were never meant to be monogamous. Animals who mate for life are certainly in the minority – only 3 per cent of mammals have lasting monogamous relationships. There may be good evolutionary reasons for this; populations are healthier when there is as much genetic diversity as possible. That is, when the male of the species spreads himself around as much as he can. Monogamy is an excellent and essential coping mechanism when a woman and child need to rely on someone to look after them. If the community or tribe as a whole don't or won't take that responsibility, and there are barriers on her doing it for herself, a strong pressure for one man to stick with one woman and his children is clearly needed. But if this is a cultural pattern, not a natural one, it's easy to see how his (and her) appetites and instincts may pull another way – hence infidelity. Another explanation could be the pressures we put on marriage and relationships today. By expecting partners to fulfil every need in each other, we set them up for disappointment and disillusionment. And it could then hardly be surprising if they look elsewhere.

Surveys suggest that the majority of men and women who are faithful do wonder at some time or other what it would be like to have an affair. If you are one of the 40 per cent of married couples in the UK who have only ever had sex with your permanent partner, before or after marrying them, you may well wonder whether sex with someone else would be better. When we read about infidelity in the media, the usual suggestion seems to be that affairs are all about sex – about passion and carnal activity. However, most people who have affairs say that poor sex with their partners is rarely the reason, and that extra marital sex itself is often worse than that enjoyed with their partners. It is from a desire to have more experience, to add a dimension missing in their relationship, and from curiosity that many stray. Others do so because of the excitement involved in deception and intrigue.

Both Jo and Roger nearly had affairs in the first years of their marriage. For Jo, the crunch point came two years after their daughter was born:

'I just felt Roger wasn't paying me any attention – he was out playing darts with his mates every other night. A friend's husband started buzzing round and I felt I mattered again. When I realised what I was about to do, I sat Roger down and said we had to talk. He was furious at first, and then he confessed he'd nearly given way to temptation too. So I said we should go to Relate, and we did.'

'I was over the moon when Jo said she was pregnant but that's when the trouble started. It was as if I was no longer needed – her Mum and sisters practically moved in and I was pushed to the side. When she had the baby, I was there for the birth but when I picked up my daughter, all I got was an endless stream of "Don't do that, hold her like this". She'd sit cuddling her for hours and I wasn't given a look in. I felt as if I could have jumped over a cliff and nobody would notice. So when this other woman made a pass at me, well, it nearly happened.'

Why do people have affairs?

Why do people have affairs? As already mentioned, it's not usually for the sex. In one survey, only one in five men having an affair said it was because of poor sex with their wives, and three out of five said they got better sex at home. Most were unfaithful because they felt neglected by their partner. Some did it because they were looking for an ego boost and the thrill of having a secret. Others did it because they were scared of making that final commitment – having a lover meant they could opt out of being really close to the person to whom they were married. Sally was married to Hamish for six years and finally had to accept he would always hold himself at arm's length:

> 'The first time Hamish was unfaithful to me was two weeks after we got back from our honeymoon. When I found out, he denied it then got tearful and swore it would never happen again. I believed him, but he did it again, and promised to change, again, a year later. In fact, I think he was being unfaithful just about six months in every year we were married. What finally did it was when he had an affair with my sister's best friend. In fact, he tried it on with my sister but she sent him packing and came straight round to tell me. I realised he'd never change and told him I'd had enough.'

There is a myth that drives many people into infidelity which is that sexual desire is irresistible. Men are prone to believe that arousal, once triggered, has to be satisfied. Women often feel the same but dress it up by calling it 'love'. As already mentioned, we do seem to believe that romantic love is some sort of 'one-off'. If you are in love with someone, the myth goes, you won't notice anyone else and nor will they be attracted to you. This isn't true, of course, but believing the myth means that when you do notice another person you may be convinced the relationship you are in is somehow a mistake or has run its course. You may become convinced that you should pursue the new one and persuade yourself that the old one is over. This can result in one person yo-yoing back and forth between two people, thoroughly confused by the fact that when they are with their lover they long to be back with their permanent partner, and vice versa. Being unfaithful may not be at all what the betraying partner wants. They feel driven inevitably to act on feelings because they didn't realise such feelings may occur and don't have to be acted on. Nevertheless, infidelity is often something that people embark upon quite deliberately. One of the reasons why one person may look outside their permanent relationship has a lot to do with making your honeymoon last. What both men and women are often looking for outside their permanent relationship is not sex and indeed not even love. What they are looking for is care.

In the early days of a relationship, both men and women acknowledge the need to be romantic. Buying presents, being thoughtful and saying loving things are all part of courting and of the early days of settling down together. Many of us think that once the dust has settled this sort of soppy behaviour can be put to rest and it's why some men and women will risk their own and their family's happiness to have an affair. The sex may be terrible because it's done hurriedly and with a guilty conscience, but what people get out of infidelity is a strong sense of being wanted and needed.

What do people get out of an affair?

Of course, having an affair can also satisfy a wish for control. Some people get a kick out of knowing that their permanent partner and their lover are being fooled and marching to the tune that only they can hear. Some people have affairs because they want to have their cake and eat it. What they are doing is splitting the two elements we have identified in a relationship – the excitement of the early phase and the security of the latter – and investing them in different people. And for some, infidelity is a way of filling in the gaps. Your partner can't satisfy every need you have – and I'm not just talking sexually here. You may share 70 or 80 per cent of your interests; both of you may have particular interests but bore each other stiff. That's where another person may come into the picture. You may not set out to find a lover who will share your fascination with stockcar racing or Japanese food; what is likely to happen is while pursuing whatever it is without your partner you meet this person who seems to understand.

If sex isn't the vital element in many relationships, what about those where it doesn't even occur? There are many partners baffled and confused because they feel as if the other half of the couple has been unfaithful, but where sex isn't part of the equation. These are the situations where their partner spends an important amount of their time or attention pursuing an interest such as golf, where clearly carnal activity has not taken place. There are also those who can swear, and do, that they haven't had sex so it's not a real affair. What may in fact be going on is that they have intense romantic entanglements with total intimacy up to and including sexual activity, but by stopping short of penetrative sex they feel that their conscience is clear. Some people having affairs insist that the effect is actually beneficial on the emotional and sexual relationship with a permanent partner. They may claim that the affair has given them confidence and increased their self-esteem. They say this helps them go back and renew their permanent relationship because they feel revitalised and pleased with themselves. Some say the sexual satisfaction they achieve in the affair helps them improve their permanent sexual relationship. The discovery and/or confession of an affair, they insist, also helps them look again at their relationship and strengthen it.

But is it true to say that affairs are good for a marriage? Any relationship counsellor will tell you that nothing is quite as painful as the discovery that your partner has betrayed you. It's often not the fact that they have had sex with someone else that hurts the most; it's the discovery that the one person you most trusted has lied and deceived you. Many people find that while it's hard to get over the realisation that your partner has had sex with someone else, it's harder still to get over the feeling that you can no longer trust them. And in a sense this fear is justified. Infidelity does not come out of nowhere, and it's nonsense to think that men or women will always have sex purely because it's offered to them and they think they can get away with it.

There is always a reason for an affair. It may happen because of influences planted way back in childhood. If a person has grown up being left and abandoned, physically or emotionally, by those they love they may have very mixed feelings about intimacy. They may believe deep down that sooner or later anyone they love will leave them. They may believe particularly that the more they love and the more vulnerable they are the more likely this is to happen. Their drive may then be to control the process and to be the one who leaves first so as not to be the one abandoned this time. They may use affairs as a way of holding love at arm's length in the belief that if they don't make the final surrender to full closeness they will be safe. Other people have affairs because of the immediate relationship. If there are unresolved problems – if there is anger, humiliation or pain that has never been dealt with – one person may wish to turn outside the relationship for reassurance even though they don't wish to end it. An affair may also seem enticing if you have been brought up to believe the myths that say monogamy is so boring. If the early days of a relationship are the only ones presented as being thrilling and satisfying it's hardly surprising that an affair may appear enticing.

Can you recover from an affair?

Can a relationship recover from an affair? The short answer has to be yes. Sometimes. It depends. Couples can learn to forgive and to rebuild their trust in each other. But forgiving is not the same as forgetting. Indeed, forgetting that an infidelity occurred means ignoring why it happened, which is not only futile but not the way to do it. The divorce courts are full of couples who tried to paper over an affair and found that it returned to haunt them. Just trying to pick up the pieces when infidelity has happened is unlikely to repair your relationship for two reasons. One is that if you don't resolve your feelings about the affair itself, you can't get over it. The person having the affair is likely to emerge from it feeling guilty, angry and confused. Rather than sweeping it under the carpet, they need to face up to why they acted as they did and how their behaviour affected their partner and other people around them. The deceived partner needs to have a chance to have their grief and anger heard and taken on board. But above all, both partners need to understand what led to the affair happening. If they don't tackle the reason for the situation, it will happen again. The one who strayed may not have another affair, but whatever emotional state led to their going outside the relationship will remain, and that in itself will create a barrier.

Couples can do the repair work themselves. What it requires is a bit of honest talking and listening. You need to hear what each of you felt in the run-up to the affair, during and after. You both need to put aside notions of blame. It doesn't help to claim that the other one, by their behaviour or feelings, caused the situation. What it needs is for each partner to own their own feelings, to explore and understand what happened, and to make changes so that it need not happen again. At the root of most infidelity is the fear of being unloved and unlovable. In most cases the way out is for both of you to pay attention to why this has happened and what you can do about it. It can be done on your own, but it is often done best with the help of a relationship counsellor. There are good reasons for this. The reason we often sweep infidelity under the carpet is because of the searingly painful emotions around it. When the subject comes up, the way we cope is by sitting on it and burying it. Talking it over can just be so awful that it often ends up in violent argument and this can spill over to all parts of our lives. What counselling does is contain everything. A counsellor helps you have the discussion openly and honestly but within the counselling room and within their protection. You can often be far more honest with each other in the presence of a counsellor than you might be on your own. What the counsellor does is to ensure this honesty does not deteriorate merely into destructive squabbling but goes some-where. You may not know how or where to begin to heal the wounds and put your relationship back together, just as you may not have the first idea of how to set a broken leg. But a professional would know, so ask for their help.

Of course, counsellors can only help you as far as you want to be helped. Sometimes, a problem is a solution. Sounds odd? Well, fighting can be a safe form of intimacy. Look back at the 'Pay-offs of fighting' section (p. 91) and you'll see that we sometimes have hidden reasons for wanting to keep a relationship hostile. Fighting can be a fast track to sexual arousal. It can be a way of keeping the emotional levels in your relationship raised. It can be a way of controlling what is going on between you. If you have doubts about your own worthiness to attract the love of someone you desire, keeping them scrapping is one way of bringing you together. Deep down, you may fear that if the fighting ended, so would the tie that binds you together. A seemingly destructive relationship may be seen as better than no relationship at all.

Don't give up

If you are experiencing problems, don't let fear or pride get in the way of seeking a solution. Counselling can help when partners may feel they don't need outside help or when people feel a relationship is without hope. It can also help even when the end result is that you stay much the way you are, but with a greater understanding of the rules that govern your own relationship.

The bottom line is that if you want your relationship to last, you have to do something. You can't be smug or blasé, you can't take it for granted. Both your partner and your partnership need to be tended, cherished and worked on. Using listening skills on each other and taking the time to sit down and talk is vital. Giving each other frequent strokes and making dates with each other really helps.

Make a date

To keep that honeymoon feeling, you need to take time out for yourself, as a couple – regularly. Many couples let the day-to-day business of living overtake their relationship. Once you are living together, especially if you make the partnership formal through marriage, it's easy to drift away from having romantic time alone together. The remedy is to make a date – once a month or, better still, once a week – to do something on your own, as a pair. Set aside some time which will be for you two on your own and don't let anything get in the way. If you keep diaries or a calendar, mark your dates on this and keep to them with the same respect as you would a date with a friend or business contact. You could use this time to treat each other to some pampering at home. Give each other a massage or a foot rub or take a bath together and scrub each other's backs. Sit and listen to some music, read or watch a programme on television that will get you talking. Or you could go out on your own, for a meal, for a drink or, if you can't afford that, for a walk. If you have children, get a baby-sitter or arrange with friends or family to give you a break so nothing can interrupt your private time.

6

Building a Better Relationship

Whether you're in the early stages of a relationship, happily partnered or facing a break-up, there are plenty of ways of forging a better relationship. We've looked at the ten stages of unravelling, the tell-tale signs that a relationship is coming apart at the seams. To balance that up, there are ten stages of knitting together – ways of forging a lasting, dynamic, exciting and sexy partnership that will keep on getting better. Whether your relationship is still 'ravelled', or whether it's beginning to go down that unhappy path, or even well on its way, you can use this process to make yourself a couple.

Ten ways you can knit your relationship together

1   Get to know each other – your pasts, your tastes, your foibles. Of course partners shouldn't live in each other's pockets, and

we all need to keep some part of ourselves separate and private. But intimacy is what brings people together, and you can only be intimate with someone you really know.

2 Set good habits in the early days. Look at all the ways you show your partner how much you love him/her, and make a promise to each other that you'll go on doing these even when the honeymoon is over. A key factor of that honeymoon feeling is that new lovers hug, kiss and hold each other all the time – not just when they're making love.

3 Once your relationship has settled into a comfortable routine, keep reminding yourself and your partner what drew you together, what attracted you to them, and the way you felt in the early days of your relationship. Focus on the positive aspects.

4 Make a point of doing something every day for your partner, and thank them out loud for anything they do that pleases you.

5 Set aside ten minutes each day to sit, face to face, with your partner and do the 'I talk, you talk' game. It could be just to tell them something that has happened to you that day. It could be to clear the air about something that has upset or hurt you.

6 Regularly see your own friends and do something that specially and specifically interests you, to maintain your own individuality and social life. But share your thoughts, your ideas and your enthusiasms with your partner so you both keep in touch with this other side of yourselves, and never keep secrets.

7 Let yourself be spontaneous. Relationships often go stale because it all becomes so predictable. If you're suddenly overcome with the urge to say 'I love you' or give them a smooch, don't hold back just because you've been married ten years or because you're standing in the queue at the supermarket. Do it, wherever or whenever. Let the moment pass and you'll get used to staying shtum, and soon both of you will get out of the habit.

8 Make a big deal out of time together. Even if money is tight and you're only spending the evening in eating sausage and mash and watching TV, make it an event. Take steps to ensure you'll be on your own, dress up and splash yourself with cologne, turn the lights low and burn candles and use the best china.

9 Look after yourself! Respect yourself and realise you are worthwhile and deserve to love and be loved.

10 'Audit' your relationship regularly, asking yourself and your partner if it's going OK and what you could do to keep yourselves up to scratch.

You need to work at it

Relationships aren't made in heaven, whatever the stories say. To make your relationship end 'happily ever after' you're going to have to do the work yourself. The sure way to finish up separating or in the divorce courts is to trust to fate, or to be smug. Either way, problems arise because you don't think you need to put any effort into making your relationship work. We've examined the obvious warning signs that suggest your relationship may be *heading* for trouble. When you don't talk to each other, when you don't seem to share time together – that's when you need to sit up and make some changes. When one of you seems to spend more time working late than being with the other, or you make excuses to be with other people, that's when you know your marriage is *in* trouble and it's really time to pull out the stops.

As well as ten ways to bring you together and give your relationship solid foundations, here are ten hints to make your relationship bombproof.

Hint 1: Don't put your head in the sand
Forget the 'happily ever after' fairy stories. You can start with the highest hopes and the best intentions. But even true love can sour and fade, if you let misunderstandings and unspoken anger take the place of communication. Accept the sad fact that relationships

can and do end – and then take steps to make sure yours won't be one of them.

Hint 2: Watch out for those 'crunch points'

Think over those points in any and every relationship when either of you may be tempted to look outside. One is when the honeymoon is over and that special spark at the start of your love affair has faded. Another is when baby makes three; and one partner may feel left out, the other that their sex appeal has gone. Yet another is when you start feeling age is creeping up, and an affair could help you feel young and desirable again. When you know your marriage could be under pressure, take extra care.

Hint 3: Make a date

If you never seem to have the time to be together, make a date. It might seem a silly thing to do if you're living together, but often the only way you're going to have the opportunity to treat each other to some tender, loving care is to pick an evening and clear away all the excuses and barriers to being alone. Remember what it was like, going out when you knew it would end in love-making and the whole evening was spent working up to that? Do it again!

Hint 4: Be honest and clear

Neither of you are mind-readers, so if you want to understand each other, you have to come out with it. If Valentine's Day, your birthday or your anniversary really matters to you, say so, and tell your partner what you'd like to do to celebrate. If you are feeling sad, angry or hurt, say so and why. Don't criticise or blame but ask your partner to see it as a shared problem to which you can both find a solution. You also need to say when you're feeling happy, loving or sexy – and invite them to help you do something about that, too!

'Roger bought me a card and flowers for Valentine's Day every year until we got married, and then it stopped', says Jo. 'For three years, I'd drop hints and hope he'd do it again and he never did.

When we went to counselling I said how much I missed him doing stuff like hugging me and holding hands, and how Valentine's Day was just the tip of the iceberg. He said he was gobsmacked – he'd never realised how I felt. Part of what we learned at counselling was telling the other what we felt. Now I'll say if I'm upset, or if I'm in a good mood, I won't take it for granted he ought to know.'

Hint 5: Plan ahead

Sit down and talk over the things you argue about most – money, chores, children. Once you know what you row about, you can agree ways of sorting it out before or as soon as it starts.

Hint 6: Don't let embarrassment get in the way

Research shows that couples who talk freely to each other about sex are half as likely to have an affair as those who don't.

Jo and Roger saw a counsellor when she realised she had very nearly given in to the temptation of an affair with a work colleague. 'She said we should get some sex books and look in them for things we'd like to try. I'd always found sex something I couldn't talk about openly – it was something we didn't mention, when I was brought up. Sex had never been very exciting with us, and this guy just flattered me. Thinking about going with him gave me such a thrill. But when Roger and I started talking about it together, I soon found sex with him could be far more of a blast than it had been, and far more exciting than a sleazy affair with someone else!'

Hint 7: Face up to your own demons

There's no point leaving one partner for another and finding yourself simply repeating the same old script. Explore what goes wrong in your relationships and why, and be prepared to take some responsibility for difficulties, and to make changes so they don't go on happening.

Hint 8: Share work as well as play
If one of you does most of the paid work and the other takes responsibility for chores around the home, you may both feel that it's a fair allotment. But if both or neither of you work outside and only one does the lion's share at home, resentment may drive a wedge between you. Talk it out between you and agree a fair division of labour.

Hint 9: Make your partner into the lover you've always wanted
Sex isn't the be-all and end-all of a relationship. Being each other's best friend is probably more important. But your sex life is often a barometer to the rest of your life together. If you're not enjoying your sex life, that may be a sign that there are gaps elsewhere. And a couple who really make the effort to be loving, passionate and exciting to each other in bed will usually find this spills over into their interactions out of bed.

Hint 10: Don't be too proud to ask for help
If you find you are having difficulties in your relationship, get help from a professional such as a counsellor. Ask for help in the early stages of needing it; don't leave it for years before going to Relate as a last resort. Try to ignore problems, and it may be too late for anyone, least of all yourselves, to rescue your relationship.

Check it out
One way of keeping your relationship both close and alive is to do an audit. This means checking it out to see how you are getting along. You can think it over by yourself or sit down with your partner and just ask 'How are we doing?' But if you're really serious about wanting yours to be a healthy relationship, you should consider doing a marital inventory. This means asking yourself a number of questions about yourself, your attitudes and how you communicate and understand each other. By looking at your own responses to various questions and talking these over with your partner, you can find the areas in your relationship that might need some discussion and attention. If you're in the early days of a

relationship, you'll find it particularly helpful to examine your relationship in this way before you tie the knot, either with marriage or by setting up home together less formally (but just as permanently). Couples who have gone through such an exercise often use what they discover about themselves, each other and the relationship to plan their future together. Doing an audit can reveal some uncomfortable truths. You may find there are important aspects of yourselves, your relationship or your lives together that you have never really talked about. If you – as many people who have done such an audit – realise there are gaps, you have three choices. You can take the opportunity to fill in the gaps and get to know each other better. You can sail on, oblivious, trusting to luck or fate. Or you can bail out before you get much further. Most people who get married spend weeks if not months planning for the wedding. Every single detail is seen as important and significant. In contrast, planning for the fifty/sixty/seventy years after the big day is often pushed aside. Which is why so many relationships get into trouble. Your relationship is more important than the initial decision or declaration that the two of you are an item. This is something the two partners should discuss and plan together, not something that should be left to luck, fate or destiny. And it's certainly not something the bride and her family arranges, but the couple itself.

The one warning that has to be made before you do an audit is that it can be strong stuff. The whole point of the exercise is to dig deep and look for the barriers to communication and understanding in your partnership. Sometimes, they're there because of something in your own background that prevents you being able to connect happily and intimately, with anyone. Sometimes, it's because of hindrances in your partner's life. Most often, it's because of the way your pasts match up and collide. This is why sharing details which seem, at first, to be trivial, can be so illuminating. It's also why delving can be explosive. You may find either or both of you feeling quite upset and angry when you look at your pasts, sometimes quite unexpectedly. You may also have to face up to the fact that you don't talk or share as well as you might like to think. Or that there are issues you skate around, and by doing so have no-go areas that could spell trouble, now or in the future. Many couples would find it reassuring and helpful to do an audit with the support and help of a trained counsellor, such as a Relate counsellor, who can guide you through and help you deal with any unexpected emotions it stirs up.

There are no wrong or right answers to a marital inventory. For instance, I might violently disagree with the statement 'A woman's place is in the home', and so might the majority of people in the twenty-first century. But if you both agree, you might be out of step with some people, but you'll have a much better relationship than if one of you agrees and one disagrees. The aim of the exercise is fourfold. One is to gain some insight into why you do and feel the way you do, by looking at your own background. Another is to see how and why you and your partner fit together. A third is to see where you differ, especially in areas you might have thought you agreed. Couples don't have to be in total accord on everything for a relationship to work. But if a multiculturalist marries a racist, there is bound to be conflict. What is important is that a couple does talk and does understand each other and broadly have some accord, tolerance and flexibility. So the fourth and most important aim of the audit is for you to use it to provoke discussion and understanding. If you think this will become a source of argument, ask for help by a counsellor in talking it through.

Tania and Owen turned down the opportunity to do an audit before their wedding because, as Tania said, 'I've got far too much to do at the moment, what with planning the big day, I can't think about anything else. Anyway, I think a little mystery is what good marriages thrive on.' Three years later, on the brink of having an affair, she approached a counsellor for help. Tania and Owen's problems appeared to centre on one main disagreement, that she wanted children as soon as possible and he did not. Whether and when to have a family had not been something they discussed before Tania had announced she was coming off the pill, two years after their wedding. Owen said he was surprised by this, as of course they hadn't wanted to have children until their business (running a small pub) was well established. She said she was surprised at his response, as of course she'd always wanted a family while they were still young. When they did an inventory, several issues surfaced at once. One was their attitude to 'family', revealed by looking at their childhood and families of origin. While Tania got on well with her parents and brother, Owen had a tricky relationship with his own family. His parents had divorced when he was ten and he refused to talk to his father, and he and his older sister argued bitterly. So while Tania had positive feelings about family and childhood, Owen's memories were of loss, pain and anger. He felt that having a family was something you had to do, but that it came with a price. Deep down, he was convinced that once a baby was on the way, Tania would switch her love and attention away from him, and their relationship would be at an end.

But the main issue was that Tania and Owen both avoided discussing anything too emotional. They only realised this when they faced up to the fact that they tended to skate around many subjects, such as money and how they actually preferred to spend their leisure time. Tania's family avoided conflict and she had a dread of raised voices and open anger. Which was why she was prone to sweep problems under the carpet, hoping that if you ignored arguments they would go away. Owen's family had open rows, but he had grown up thinking that the end result of rows was separation and loss. Tania remembered her childhood as idyllic, but then confronted a memory she had always tried to avoid: that her parents very nearly separated soon after she and her brother left home. Doing the inventory and discussing the results was painful for both of them, but it resulted in a greater understanding of why they behaved and felt the way they did. Tania and Owen emerged from their audit with a far stronger, closer and more intimate relationship.

Doing your audit

First, fill each other in about your family and your own background. Answer these questions:

What is your age and date of birth?

Did you have brothers and/or sisters?

If you said yes, how many brothers and/or sisters?

Where did you come in the family (i.e. middle child, older brother of two sisters, younger sister of one of each, etc.)?

Did your birth parents stay together or were they separated divorced?

If your parents split up, did you have a step-parent/step-siblings?

What contact did you have with your mother's/father's parents and other relatives?

Did you experience any deaths in your family while growing up?

How did your family celebrate festivals such as Christmas, Diwali, Al-Hijra or Rosh Hashanah?

Did you have any further education or vocational training?

Did your family have pets?

Did you own/were you responsible for an animal while growing up?

Did your family move house/area while you were growing up?

Did your family go away on holidays when you were growing up?

Where did your family go away on holidays when you were growing up?

What is the worst thing that happened to you when you were growing up?

What is the best thing that happened to you when you were growing up?

How/when/why did you leave home?

Were you expected to do chores when you were growing up?

How old were you when you met your partner?

Then, have a look at these statements and, separately, each record your response.

What did you expect from your relationship?

	No, NO!	No	Not sure	Yes	Yes, YES!
On the whole, I'm happy with our relationship.					
Sometimes I wish we could be the way we were when we first met.					
I often think other couples are happier than we are.					
Time is not going to change us or our relationship.					
We're everything to each other and don't need other people.					
I'll never be attracted to anyone else again.					
My partner only has eyes for me.					
If you really love each other, most problems can be overcome.					
A good relationship comes naturally.					
I'm sure our relationship will be happier when we get married.					

	No, NO!	No	Not sure	Yes	Yes, YES!
I'm sure our relationship will be happier when we have kids.					
I'm sure our relationship will be happier when we move house.					
I'm sure our relationship will be happier when we have more money.					

Is your partner someone you like?

I like my partner's character.					
My partner often does things that please me or make me happy.					
My partner often does things that annoy or upset me.					
There is nothing about my partner I'd like to change.					
My partner is different with me than with other people.					
There are some aspects of my partner I always hoped would change or thought I could change.					
I think my partner has changed in the time I've known them.					

Do you communicate with each other?

	No, NO!	No	Not sure	Yes	Yes, YES!
We talk to each other about our feelings.					
We often don't have to talk, we just know what the other is thinking.					
I always know what my partner is feeling about important issues.					
I'm happy to tell my partner how I feel.					
I always tell my partner what I think.					
My partner listens to me when I talk to him/her.					
I can tell my partner anything.					
We don't talk enough.					
I sometimes feel my partner doesn't listen to me.					
My partner interrupts me when I try to talk to him/her.					
My partner can do things that surprise me.					

	No, NO!	No	Not sure	Yes	Yes, YES!
Everyone should have some secrets and keep some mystery.					
When my partner is unhappy I usually know why.					
When I'm unhappy I can usually tell my partner why.					
There are certain subjects we avoid talking about.					
I feel close to my partner.					
Least said, soonest mended.					

Can you settle arguments?

When we disagree, we can usually talk things over and come to an understanding.					
When we disagree, one of us always gets their way.					
We don't argue.					
We often disagree but nothing changes.					
I find myself avoiding bringing up certain things in case it leads to a row.					

	No, NO!	No	Not sure	Yes	Yes, YES!
Sometimes I feel scared about my partner's reactions.					
I hate raised voices.					
When we have a disagreement it always ends in a fight.					
My partner can't take criticism or accept blame.					
I find it hard to apologise.					
We have the same argument time after time.					
Our rows simmer on for ages and get brushed under the carpet without a proper ending.					

Can you agree on money management?

We both know what the other one earns.					
I don't always tell my partner the real cost of something I've bought.					
We sometimes argue about money.					

	No, NO!	No	Not sure	Yes	Yes, YES!
When bills come in, we talk them over and know how much we're spending.					
We plan our spending together.					
We agree about what we spend our money on.					
We're getting into debt because we spend more than we have coming in.					
Money is for spending.					
I worry about having enough to get by.					
Men usually earn more than women.					

What do you do in your spare time?

I have friends I like seeing on my own.					
I enjoy spending time with my partner.					
We have similar tastes in how to spend our spare time.					
I feel insecure when one of us is spending time away.					

170

	No, NO!	No	Not sure	Yes	Yes, YES!
My partner is happy to join me doing something I enjoy.					
We spend about the right time doing things together.					
We spend about the right time doing things separately.					
We never have enough leisure time.					

Is your sex life satisfying?

I'm comfortable talking about sex.					
We have sex as often as I'd like.					
I always have an orgasm.					
When we have sex, I enjoy it.					
We talk about sex in a general way.					
I feel confident about my sexual knowledge.					
I know what makes me sexually aroused and satisfied.					
I know what makes my partner sexually aroused and satisfied.					

	No, NO!	No	Not sure	Yes	Yes, YES!
I've been able to tell my partner what makes me sexually aroused and satisfied.					
There are sex acts I'd like to try but I haven't been able to say so.					
There are sex issues I'd like to talk about with my partner.					
I would never be unfaithful.					
My partner would never be unfaithful.					
If one of us were unfaithful, the relationship would be finished.					

Having children

We have talked about having children.					
I know how many children I want and when.					
I know how many children my partner wants and when.					
We have the same ideas on how to bring up children.					

	No, NO!	No	Not sure	Yes	Yes, YES!
We both have the same attitudes to disciplining and smacking children.					
A man can look after children just as well as a woman.					
We've discussed and agreed which responsibilities each of us will take on when we have children.					
A relationship isn't complete unless there are children.					
Having a child shows how much you love someone.					

Family matters

I get on with my partner's parents and other members of their family.					
I have good relationships with members of my family.					
I get on well with my friends.					
I get on well with my partner's friends.					
We have people who are friends of both of us.					

	No, NO!	No	Not sure	Yes	Yes, YES!
My friends are important to me.					
The amount of time we see friends and family is about right.					
I feel very positive about my relationships with friends and family.					
I feel close to my family.					

Who does what?

When it comes to making big decisions, we talk them over and agree together.					
We agree on how to share chores and responsibilities fairly so neither of us feels hard done by.					
There are some things that are men's work and some that are women's.					
Sometimes we argue about who does and decides what.					
We've talked it over and it doesn't matter which of us is the major breadwinner.					

	No, NO!	No	Not sure	Yes	Yes, YES!
We've agreed how we are going to divide work and child-care responsibilities.					
Housework is mainly women's work.					

Political, social and religious beliefs

We have similar religious beliefs.					
We agree on what's right and wrong.					
I respect my partner's beliefs.					
I know which political party my partner supports.					
We have the same political views.					
We talk about our political beliefs.					
Sometimes I disagree with my partner's views on society.					

Your sex life

A good sexual relationship is important to a lasting partnership. It isn't the quantity of sex you have but the quality of sex you enjoy that adds to your life. Once the honeymoon is over, sex can take a back seat to other aspects of your life together. If there are jobs that have to be done, family that has to be looked after, the sexual side of your partnership may seem a luxury you can't afford. Desire and sexual activity are often put on hold for those occasions when we think we may have time – weekends or holidays. The problem is that when these do come around, we're often too preoccupied or tired to take advantage, or, worst of all, we've become so accustomed to not bothering that we continue to do so. But if your partner, and your love life, keep being brushed aside, one day you may wake up to find your relationship in trouble. If you want to keep a relationship alive you need to make time for each other as a couple, and make an effort both to keep your sex life alive and developing. It often helps to have specific suggestions for putting the sparkle back into a love affair gone stale.

Sex lives often go stale because:

- you're too tired
- you haven't the time
- you haven't the privacy
- you don't feel like it.

Ali and Nina had been together for five years when they realised their marriage was having problems. They seemed to argue all the time and both were wondering whether to call it a day. A friend suggested a second honeymoon and they decided to play it for real. They booked into the same hotel, asking for the same suite they had when they got married. They revisited the places and did everything they'd done the first time round. They found themselves remembering exactly what it was they had felt in the early days of their marriage and what they had done to keep it going. 'I realised I'd stopped listening to Nina,' says Ali. 'We'd just got used to taking each other for granted,' agrees Nina. 'Married life had got so dull, it wasn't like the fun we'd had in the first days. We hardly ever had sex, and when we did it, it was a case of do the same things as usual and get it over with quickly. What that holiday helped us see was that sex and our marriage could be just as exciting as it was on holiday all the time, we'd only ourselves to blame for letting it go stale.' Now Nina and Ali have a tryst once a month with each other. They meet up in the bar where they had their first date, and pretend to pick each other up. Having to make the effort to act as if they're new to each other keeps them on their toes.

Too tired?

Being too tired to spend private time with your partner is often a case of priorities or stress management. Either you allow other, ultimately less, important issues to take up most of your attention and energy, or you let yourself become so tense and strung out that even given time alone, you're too uptight to enjoy it. There is a third reason, that there are underlying problems which you're trying to ignore. If you turn your back on issues that are coming between you, your own mind may use tiredness or illness as a way of trying to attract your attention. Either way, you need to take action.

If it's priorities

Sit down with your partner and brainstorm around your day-to-day and week-to-week activities. What takes up your time and your energy, and prevents you having a love life together? Divide your time into things you have to do, things you should do, things you choose to do and things that could be postponed. Be realistic about what goes into the first category. Anything else is up for discussion. Which would you both agree to put to one side in order to have some time, and energy, to spend on each other?

If it's stress

Have a long and honest look at your lifestyle. Are you stressed? Are there responsibilities you take on that you don't have to make your own? Stress management means examining the things that get you worked up and looking at ways of bringing down your anxieties. Sometimes, this means accepting that you aren't indispensable – your family or colleagues can be asked to do things that up to now you've insisted only you can manage.

If it's underlying issues

You and your partner may need to find out why one or both of you are using tiredness to avoid each other. You may need to use the ideas already suggested in this book – particularly genograms and relationship maps – to see what could be affecting your ability to communicate. You may find 'What's this about' in chapter 3 helps you understand what is going on, and wrong, between you. 'I' messages and feelings exercises could be helpful to put you in touch again.

Haven't the time?

It's worth spending money and effort to be on your own. Whatever the reason, you may need to adjust your schedule to allow for private time when you can make room for a love life. There is nothing wrong with setting aside a few hours, as often as you want, to make whoopee. It isn't perverted, abnormal, juvenile, unusual or im-moderate. What often stops you is the belief that sex is special and different, and somehow not an integral part of your life or your relationship. A happy sex life is seen as a cherry on the cake, an extra that we can do without. In fact, sex is a part of sexual health. That doesn't mean that if you aren't having sex three times a week you're worse off than someone who is, or that having sex three times a day confers joy. What it means is that if you aren't enjoying the sex life you and your partner would really like – whether it's twice a month or twice a day – you and your relationship are likely to suffer. So it really is important to set aside time to please yourselves, and know it is doing you good. If you have children, establish a rule that there are times when Mum and Dad are to be left alone except for serious injury or life-and-death situations. They can sleep, read or watch the box perfectly well on their own without disturbing you for two hours. If you think this is unreasonable, dangerous or embarrassing, send the family off for a few hours to friends, family or some form of child-care or activity so you can concentrate totally on each other. Use the time to treat each other.

A sexy interlude

Spread some towels on your bed – or living room floor or patio or wherever takes your fancy. Lie down with your partner and take a generous handful of oil or cream and spread it all over each other, gently massaging wherever it feels good. Take it in turns to kiss and stroke your partner's body from toes to lips and back again. Then concentrate on the sexy bits – but ask your partner which bits they best like being touched, and whether they want it slow and gentle or firm and fast. Only when you've covered each other's bodies with kisses and strokes, and are both in a lather to go on, move into having full sex.

Haven't the privacy?

If you have children or share your living arrangements with other people, it can sometimes be difficult to be alone together with no interruptions. Whatever other people's expectations or feelings are, make your own rules about this and stick to them. Insist that there are certain times when you have privacy to be alone – whether you use that time to talk, just spend time in each other's company or make love. Even young children will learn to respect the concept of personal time and space, especially if you make it a trade and respect theirs too.

Don't feel like it?

Everyone's sex life can go a bit stale, but it's more than possible to kick-start yours back on track again. Here are six things to do in bed that will transform your sex life – for ever.

Make a list

Write down the ten things you'd really like your partner to do for you, romantically or sexually. Your requests can range from 'Tell me how nice I look' or 'Say you love me', to 'Spend at least ten minutes stroking my nipples with a feather', and 'Let's try some oral sex'! Ask him/her to come up with a list for themselves, and then do one each for each other, tonight.

Try a new lovemaking position

Are you always the one underneath, staring at the ceiling and wondering whether it's time to decorate again, or the one on top wondering why your bed linen is sooooo boring? Roll your partner over and get a new perspective. A different sexual position can give you more than a fresh view. Some sexual positions – particularly women-on-top and on all-fours, doggy fashion – are especially good for female sexual pleasure. When she's in the driving seat, she can vary the angle of penetration, the depth and speed of thrusts to ensure her own satisfaction. If he's entering from behind, both partners can use their fingers to caress her clitoris to make sure she is aroused and satisfied. He benefits too – both positions are far less tiring for the man so he can keep going longer. Trying out new positions for making love is certain to add a little extra spice to your love life.

Try a new place or time

Love lives can get stuck in a rut if you always know where and when – in bed, after lights out – you're going to make love. I'm not suggesting you take the Beatles at their word ('Why don't we do it in the road?'), but being a little daring and different can work wonders. If you have a garden, sneak out at midnight and make love in the open air, under the stars. If you don't, take a day-trip to somewhere wild and remote. Or try the delights of the kitchen table, living room floor, bathroom or stairs. Set your clock an hour early and try an early morning kiss-and-cuddle, or have a siesta mid-morning or afternoon.

Slow, slow, quick, quick, slow

There are times when long, slow love-making is best. But in the early days of your relationship, there might have been times when you were gasping for it and couldn't wait. Recapture the excitement of honeymoon times by giving in to impulse and having the occasional quickie. If you would like to make love, but hesitate, telling yourself 'We're just about to go out/we've just got home/ should be making a meal – we'll do it later', hold that thought. Half the time, you won't, and the moment will pass. So make love *now*.

A little thrill and chill

There's nothing like a fright to get the juices flowing. Do something scary today – visit a theme park and go on a white-knuckle ride, have a walk at midnight together, fish that spider out of the bath yourself. Share the shivers, then share a cuddle to make you feel better – and see where it leads!

Dream lover

We all have sexual fantasies, and they brighten up our secret, personal sex lives. You can really bring the honeymoon back into a love life by trying some for real. Next time you make love, tell your partner what you'd love to do to them in your fantasies – have sex on a deserted tropical beach, have them do a strip, cover each other in chocolate and lick it off. Just describing it can bring back the spark between you. If yours is a fantasy you could act out – such as one of you dressing up as a French Maid and having the other tickle you with your feather duster – agree to try it out.

Super Genie

Making your honeymoon last and having a dynamic, vital, strong, adaptable and happy relationship isn't an unreasonable request. It is, however, unrealistic to expect it to fall into your lap at the wave of a magic wand and for you to live 'happily ever after' just like that. But, if we are going to be talking about this in fairy story terms, let's for a second imagine there is a Genie who could grant your wishes. S/he's a modern Genie, however. S/he demands, like any good counsellor or agony aunt, that you do most of the work yourselves. In recompense, you're allowed double the number of wishes usually allotted in the old tales. So – six wishes from the

Super Genie, for a relationship that will last well into the new millennium.

I'd like to understand my feelings.
You'll need to recognise who you fall in love with and why. You'll need to learn about the influence of your childhood and your family on your emotions and your ability to make relationships. Go back to chapter 1 and learn how.

I'd like us to learn to communicate.
You'll need to equip yourselves with the skills of talking and listening. You'll need to learn how to give feelings a name, to accept them, to do 'I' messages. Go back to chapter 2 and learn how.

I'd like to resolve arguments before we say things we'd regret.
You'll need to understand why you argue and what about and to learn the techniques of constructive disagreement. Go back to chapter 3 and learn how.

I don't want our life to change.
No deal! But Super Genie can help you understand why change is necessary and how, when and why it happens. You can learn to see when change is likely to happen in virtually every relationship and to see when, why and how you need to pay special attention. Go back to chapter 4 and learn how.

I'd like to learn how to solve our problems.
All relationships go through problematical stages. There are ways to tell when a relationship is sliding towards danger, and ways both to recognise the warning signs and to take steps to repair the problems. Go back to chapter 5 and learn how.

I'd like the perfect relationship.
Wouldn't we all! Perfection is unrealistic but you can aspire to and achieve Good Enough. Chapter 6 has tips on knitting your relationship together, making it bombproof and putting a sparkle back

into your sex life. Go back to the beginning of this chapter and learn how.

The end – a beginning

In order to *Make Your Honeymoon Last* you do need to embrace the ups as well as the downs, and take the rough with the smooth. But if you do this, you will realise you don't have to bail out of a relationship as soon as it begins to be familiar to keep the magic alive in your life. As Mae West was supposed to have said, 'It's not the men in your life but the life in your men', and that applies to relationships as well. Go for quality instead of quantity, put the effort into keeping the sparkle in what you have instead of looking again for something different, and you will put your relationship on the best possible footing. Welcome to the twenty-first century – and welcome to your new, lasting, honeymoon relationship!

Further Help

National

UK

Many doctors' practices now offer a counsellor or you can find one at your local family planning clinic – their address will be in your local phone book, or ring the **fpa**'s Helpline on 020 7837 4044.

British Association for Counselling can suggest a counsellor in your area. You can ring them on 01788 550899 or write to **BAC**, 1 Regent Place, Rugby, Warks CV21 2PJ.

Couples Counselling Network can also offer telephone counselling for the price of a phone call and may be able to refer you on to a counsellor in your neighbourhood. Their Helpline is on 08700 763376.

Relate can help with any relationship worries, including sexual problems. Look in the local phone book for your nearest centre.

fpa have a range of leaflets and mail order books on all aspects of sex, sexuality and contraception and can give you information on local services. Ring the Helpline on 020 7837 4044, or write to 2–12 Pentonville Road, London N1 9FP.

Issue offers help to couples having problems conceiving. Their address is 114 Lichfield Street, Walsall WS1 1SZ. Tel: 01922 722888.

Association for Post-Natal Illness advises and supports women suffering from post-natal depression. Contact them at 25 Jerdan Place, London SW6 1BE. Tel: 020 7386 0868.

ParentLine Plus gives support and telephone counselling to anyone in a parenting situation, whether you're married and whether or not the kids live with you full-time, whatever the worry or anxiety. Their freephone Helpline is on 0808 800 2222. You can also write to them at 520 Highgate Studios, 53–79 Highgate Road, Kentish Town, London NW5 1TL, or e-mail them at headoffice@parentlineplus.org.uk.

Impotence Association gives help for men suffering from erectile dysfunction, and also to their partners. Contact them on their Helpline, 020 8767 7791, or write to Impotence Association, PO Box 10296, London SW17 9WH.

International

Australia

Family planning

Family Planning Australia (National Office)
9/114 Maitland Street
Hackett, ACT 2602
Tel: [+61] (02) 6230 5255
Fax: [+61] (02) 6230 5344
E-mail: fpa@actonline.com.au

Infertility

Access
PO Box 959
Parramatta, NSW 2124
Tel: [+61] (02) 9670 2380
Fax: [+61] (02) 9670 2608

Fertility Society of Australia
ACTS, GPO Box 2200
Canberra, ACT 2601
Tel: [+61] (02) 6257 3299
Fax: [+61] (02) 6257 3256
A.C.N. 006 214 115

On the Internet, you can also find information about infertility at
www.ein.org

Post-natal Depression

Post and Ante Natal Depression Association (PaNDa)
1st Fl, Canterbury Family Ctr.
19 Canterbury Road
Camberwell, Victoria 3124
Tel: [+61] (03) 9882 5396
Fax: [+61] (03) 9813 3927
E-mail: panda@vicnet.net.au

On the Internet, you can also find international and local help and information at www.pregnancy.about.com

Relationship Counselling

Relationships Australia (National Office)
15 Napier Close, Deakin ACT 2600
PO Box 313, Curtin ACT 2605
Tel: [+61] (02) 6285 4466
Fax: [+61] (02) 6285 4722
E-mail: national_office@relationships.com.au

USA

Family Planning

Planned Parenthood Federation of America
810 Seventh Ave.
New York, NY 10019
Tel: [+1] (212) 541 7800
Fax: [+1] (212) 245 1845
E-mail: communications@ppfa.org
Website: www.plannedparenthood.org

Impotence

Impotents Anonymous and **I-ANON**. Call [+1] (800) 669 1603 for information on local support groups. Call [+1] (800) 867 7042 for names of physicians in your area who have special interest in treating impotence.

Impotence Information Center
PO Box 9
Minneapolis, MN 55440
Tel: [+1] (800) 843 4315

Impotence Institute of America
8201 Corporate Drive
Suite 320
Landrover, MD 20785
Tel: [+1] (301) 577 0650

Sexual Function Health Council
American Foundation for Urologic Disease
300 West Pratt Street
Suite 401
Baltimore, MD 21201
Tel: [+1] (800) 242 2383

On the Internet, you can also find discussion groups and newsgroups such as www.alt.support.impotence

Infertility

The American Infertility Association
666 Fifth Avenue
Suite 278
New York, NY 10103
E-mail: info@americaninfertility.org

On the Internet, you can also find information about infertility at www.ein.org

Post Natal (Post Partum) Depression

Depression After Delivery (DAD)
PO Box 1282
Morrisville, PA 19067
Tel: [+1] (800) 944 4773

Postpartum Support, International
927 North Kellogg Avenue
Santa Barbara, CA 93111
Tel: [+1] (805) 967 7636

On the Internet, you can also find international and local help and information at www.pregnancy.about.com

Relationships

Association of Couples for Marriage Enrichment
459 South Church Street
PO Box 10596
Winston-Salem, North Carolina 27108

American Association for Marriage and Family Therapy
PO Box 79445
Baltimore, MD 21279-0445
Website: www.aamft.org

National Council on Family Relations
3989 Central Avenue NE
Suite 550
Minneapolis, MN 55421

On the Internet, you can also find information about relationships at www.ivillage.com/relationships

Index

Other Help Yourself titles:

Come Alive
Your Six Point Plan for Lasting Health and Energy

Beth MacEoin

Do you feel below par most of the time, not ill enough to
visit your GP, but lacking the energy and vitality you need to
live life to the full, looking and feeling your best? *Come Alive*
offers a six point plan which is radical yet achievable and which
cuts through much of the current advice on health issues which
can seem confusing, contradictory or downright impossible.

- How to boost your physical, mental and emotional energy
- How to strengthen your immune system in mind and body
- How to adopt an eating plan that is delicious and healthy
- How to exercise enough for great fitness with minimum effort
- How to value relaxation and positive thinking
- How to limit the damage when life goes off the rails

Published by Hodder & Stoughton
ISBN 0 340 74582 7

Feel Fabulous Over Fifty

Gloria Hunniford and Jan de Vries

Good health and maximum energy are crucial at every age, but perhaps it is in the approach to fifty that we really begin to assess our lifestyles for the longer term benefits. Gloria Hunniford and Jan de Vries have worked together for ten years on health programmes for the BBC and believe that there is no reason why we should not enjoy great fitness and good health into our fifties and beyond. Indeed, it is never too late to adopt a healthy approach and make the fifties our best years yet!

- How do I look?
- How do I feel?
- How do I cope with the menopause?
- How do I care for my skin and hair?
- How do I drink and eat healthily?
- How do I exercise?
- How do I keep my love life active?

Published by Hodder & Stoughton
ISBN 0 340 74594 0

Get the Happiness Habit

How You Can Choose Your Steps to a Happy Life

Christine Webber

Happiness is a natural force within us. But sometimes we have to relearn it. It seems that at some point in our lives we lose the gift of being happy and are constantly struggling to find that elusive joy. This inspiring book discourages the illusion that happiness can be bought or acquired or will magically happen. Instead it shows that happiness is an inner choice and that with a bit of skill and a mind shift, life will never be the same again.

- Assess your own happiness
- Learn the secrets of happy people
- Rethink those irrational, negative beliefs
- Stop feeling guilty
- Know that you deserve to be happy
- Act happy – be happy

Published by Hodder & Stoughton
ISBN 0 340 74593 2

Make Love Work for You

An Essential Guide for Career Couples

Julia Cole

When both partners work, great pressures can be put on the relationship, usually because of stress and its negative effects, different work patterns and expectations, and the complexities of child-care. Julia Cole deals with all these issues and many more, and shows that dual careers can be stimulating and rewarding if the issues are addressed positively.

- Who does the domestic chores?
- What if one partner is a workaholic?
- How to manage your time together and apart
- Need your sex life suffer?
- How can you support each other without feeling competitive or resentful?
- How to cope with common gender stereotypes
- What happens if children come along?

Published by Hodder & Stoughton
ISBN 0 340 74595 9